Zilla,
Thank you
for your kind
editing.
You are my favourite
poet.

Love,
Diana

xxx ♡
ooo

Promise of Angels

Diana Michael

Cover Design: SelfPubBookCovers.com/RLSather
Star Chapter Design: Made by Freepik from www.flaticon.com
ISBN: 978-0692774632

10 9 8 7 6 5 4 3 2 1

Printed in the United States of America

Promise of Angels

A miraculous, true story of hope.
Making LIGHT of the spiritual journey.

Diana Michael

Monarchangel Ink

This book is dedicated to God for keeping the Light in me through the darkness.

Disclaimer

The information in this book is intended to be entertaining and informational in promoting wellness; it is not intended as medical advice or to replace the advice or services of a medical physician. Before undertaking any self-care regimen or "complementary" therapy, it is advisable to consult a physician, especially pertaining to healthcare needs that require a medical diagnosis. The author and publisher are not responsible for any adverse effects resulting from seeking alternative therapies.

All the stories of healing are true and anecdotal. Many names have been changed because of preference or inability to contact the participants.

Contents

Foreword

It is a small miracle that I learned about Diana Michael—through a woman I met by chance, named Beth. The improbable meeting was on the tarmac of the Philadelphia airport. I was heading to Minnesota to give an integrative medicine presentation at Mayo Clinic, but my plane seemed headed nowhere. After finally getting in the air, it was clear that my connection in Chicago was at risk. I prayed, "God, I trust you. Thy will, not my will, be done."

On arrival in Chicago, I raced to catch my connection. The door leading down to the plane had closed, and no amount of banging would change that. Nearby, a woman cried; the missed flight meant she would get little time visiting her sons. The two of us sat in the back seat of the next plane to Minnesota. Beth, a gifted healer as God so planned it, shared a wealth of miraculous spiritual stories ideal for my new book, *God's House Calls*. Beth had also touched Diana's life—our connection.

Four years ago, if I had read Diana's new book, it would have been too incredible to believe. After twenty-three years of formal education culminating in a family medicine specialty, my left-brain mushroomed while my right brain shrank. Despite a strong Christian upbringing, and wishing God existed, it was difficult to comprehend.

That began changing when I approached fifty. I yearned to learn how I could live a long, healthy life. After dozens of national integrative health conferences and 10,000 hours of study in nutritional, botanical, functional, integrative, genetic and holistic medicine, a completely different perspective arose. Now, instead of pushing medicine to get patients well, I stop administering medicine as quickly as I can and switch to much safer, more effective remedies. Integrative holistic conferences led me to an understanding of quantum physics and associated energy medicine.

My patients began to share personal and profound experiences with me. I was honored to have their trust. Three years ago, a patient shared how her blissful near-death experience transformed her life. "The other realm is more real than this one." She didn't want to come back. She had a "knowing" about God and no longer feared death. An alcoholic had a negative near-death experience, turned his life around, and then had a blissful one. Another, after two near-death experiences, became gifted and gives me spiritual guidance. Spiritual experiences began showing up in my own life. My patients have now shared over 300 experiences—premonitions, intuitions, out-of-body experiences, voices and visions—that acquainted them with God; it focused them on their mission for the world. Stories privately shared by these upbeat, serene individuals, whom I would want as my best friends, have led me to a great revelation: God is not only real, God is so big, so incredible, so loving and so powerful that we can never come close to a full understanding. God cannot and will not fit in the box we have built for Him.

My mission was to write a book destigmatizing these experiences that too often are kept secret. I was to let individuals know that the Bible is not only metaphorical; miracles, angels and healing are literal. Others agreed, reading the accounts in my book, *God's House Calls*, and making it #1 on Amazon in four categories (www.godshousecalls.com).

Diana was raped at age sixteen and indoctrinated with religious guilt and shame. She had a chronically ill, reclusive mother. Her life began with major challenges that brought her close to death many times. This book, full of so many unbelievable surprises, resonated with me deeply because of the experiences my patients shared. I was awakened to the grace of Divine intervention. God loves children; time and again, God gifts those not yet grown who have experienced major tragedy or hardship. Diana's life was touched—by angels—with a promise.

Our ultimate rewards in life are directly correlated with the severity of our challenges. We must experience hate to appreciate love, hardship to appreciate plenty, rejection to create solutions. Creativity is born from conflict.

Now when I hear "That is not possible!" I understand that,

through God, anything is possible. Diana's life has been a steep rollercoaster. When she hit bottom, she wisely was advised to focus on helping others. Her challenges, good deeds and perseverance have led to a life that has been incredibly blessed. It opens a magnificent window to understanding God's omnipotence and how God works so incredibly through those who do His work.

This book is a testament of hope for those who feel their life has no meaning or their suffering is in vain. Truly it is a testament to God's love; never underestimate its power and how it can manifest. Life can be about awe, gratitude, forgiveness, service and love. Diana, thank you for courageously sharing your story that is such a bright beacon for our own lives.

Jim Roach MD, ABIHM, ABFM

"Man tries to measure the ocean of knowledge with the cup of his mind."

\- Anonymous

Preface

When I was a teenager, I took an overdose of medication that could stop an elephant's heart. Two magnificent angels escorted me out of my body in flight to an ethereal conference room with a large, oblong table in the center. Figures of light were seated there—angels, spirit guides, ancestors, and familiar souls. On the other side, I did not hear with my ears but communicated telepathically, effortlessly. I knew the angels' thoughts, and they knew mine.

Suddenly, a white sheet of paper floated slowly down onto the table. Letters appeared one by one on the blank paper, spelling T-R-U-T-H. Just as quickly as I had left my dying body, the angels escorted me back. In their presence, I felt a deep, unquestionable, Divine Love. There was no way I was going back into that tortured teenage body and mind, but I knew my contract with this physical form was not yet up. The urging had been less a gentle "Return if you wish" and more a stern "Get back down there." I reluctantly sank back into the density of the third dimension. The angels vowed to protect me and asked that I tell the truth. I had no idea who or what they would protect me from or what truth I was to tell.

I was unconscious for six weeks. I forgot everything I had experienced until I retrieved the memory later in hypnosis, but two things changed: I was no longer suicidal—even though the worst part of my life was yet to come—and I was obsessed with writing. Looking back, I see I was protected from death many times. This true story is written in letters to Penny, my friend who passed away from cancer. She always encouraged me to keep writing. It has been my obsession to tell the truth and give hope to others in return for the *Promise of Angels*.

Chapter 1

A Boob on My Eye and a Butterfly

Dear Penny,

You died from cancer a year ago today. I miss you. Bill and I had a shot of Bailey's Irish Cream in our morning coffee and toasted your spirit. We went to downtown Anoka, the neighboring town where you lived, and walked by your favorite haunts, ending our hike at the site where the Mississippi River and the Rum River meet. This is an eerie January in Minnesota without snow. It was fifty-two degrees today, when it is usually five degrees below zero. I wore the leopard underwear you gave me when I had surgery. I smile when I wear it—but I'm getting ahead of myself.

Being rescued by angels wasn't the first time my life was saved—or the last. When angels rescue you from death, they don't stop all your troubles. My death was postponed again last summer. For years, I had a little bump above my left eye near my eyebrow: a whitehead that I squeezed exudate out of. Last August, when I did my usual squeeze, the lump got bigger. The next day it swelled up and had a raised white center that resembled a nipple. I commented to my husband Bill that I had a boob on my eye. I squeezed it again and my entire eye swelled up. I went to bed that night, expecting it to be better by morning. When I woke up, I had a skin bag of fluid hanging under my left eye and my right eye was also swelling up. I looked like a monster. My family doctor told me it was an infected sebaceous cyst. I was given antibiotics and warned to have the root surgically removed or it would grow back. That day, the doctor pushed me to get an overdue mammogram. After the boob on my eye was removed, I got my breasts smashed. There was a malignant tumor—but this is not about cancer. It is just how the story begins.

For decades I had irregular mammograms that scared the

crap out of me, and they were always benign cysts. Finally, after years of avoiding mammograms, the boob on my eye forced me to get another. It felt as though the intrusive eye of the x-ray scanner, determined to find cancer, finally got what it wanted. I was grateful it was found and I could get treatment. I wondered if the placebo effect doctors learned about in medical school worked the opposite way. If patients who received sugar pills but believed they received drugs were cured, could patients who believe they will get cancer and consistently search for it create malignancy? Medicine has a name for this, too; it is called the "nocebo effect." It illustrates how powerful your beliefs are and how incredibly important the words doctors use are—especially in oncology.

When I found out I had cancer, I was volunteering at the Cancer Resource Center doing hands-on healing/Qigong with cancer patients. Penny, you were dealing with cancer, too. I remember when I met you twenty years ago at a clinic where I worked; you were getting treatment for thymus cancer. Later you had breast cancer caused by the earlier radiation treatment. We were still friends but didn't see each other more than twice a year until you came to my house for a hands-on-healing treatment.

When it became obvious your time was running out, I went to your apartment to do healing and we became very close. In twenty-five years of doing healing, I seldom received healing for myself, but with my cancer diagnosis I immediately requested to be put on half a dozen prayer and healing lists for distance healing. During the next two months I felt the healing energy lifting my spirit, diminishing my fear.

The week before my surgery, I was in the garden in front of our home, cutting the last zinnias of September. A small black butterfly with orange-and-white markings flew around me and landed on my breast, literally alight on the tumor, in an awkward place on the left side. I stood breathless in the sunlight, like in a dream, not wanting to disturb my visitor. It stayed for several minutes. I knew exactly what kind of butterfly it was: a Red Admiral. I had just read *Messages*, a book about spirit visitations to 9/11 survivors, and one story involved that butterfly. Penny, when I told you what happened, you said, "That's my butterfly" and shared with me that a few weeks earlier you were sitting outside on a lawn chair and the same kind of butterfly landed on your mastectomy site and stayed for over half an hour. You thought it might be the spirit of the baby girl you lost when she was six months old. After that, we were butterfly sisters. You almost died three times last January. Then on your trip to California you passed away on the plane, halfway to heaven. Eerily, my brother-in-law was on that flight that was diverted to bring your body back to earth.

Last spring, I went to visit Gina Booth, a psychic I had never met before. At the end of the reading, she said the spirit of a woman was there to visit me—had been bugging her throughout the reading. Gina said the ethereal visitor had died with pressure in her ears and head and then her heart gave out. That is what happened to you on the plane from the cabin pressure. In spirit, you were holding a stack of papers which I recognized as a book manuscript. You were pain free and ecstatic. You told Gina that I needed to "get going" on my writing or you'd "kick my butt." Gina said you held my face in your hands, thanked me and said you would help me if I called on you.

Penny, you know I have the best husband (my first not so much). Ever since he had prostate cancer I've been afraid of being without him. I am sending God mixed messages: "Heal me, and get me out of here first!"

The lumpectomy went quickly and I was sent home the day of surgery. The margins were clear and it had not spread to my lymph nodes. Five years post-surgery, my last mammogram was clear. Bill has been cancer free for ten years. Medicine may have saved my life, but what gave me hope and comfort was energy healing. The oncologist believes you are "in remission" until the cancer returns. After frantically searching the Internet for cancer cures, the overwhelming message was just as discouraging: nearly everything you eat, drink and breathe may be carcinogenic. I didn't have the time, the money or the energy to avoid everything toxic. However, I met a woman last year who'd had a cancerous tumor the size of a softball, which she claimed disappeared with a pure natural diet, supplements and natural healing methods. She did coffee enemas. I prefer to drink my latte.

In the movie *Touch of Hope,* a famous healer in a research project placed his hand over a covered dish filled with cancer cells; several malignant cells died and floated to the top of the dish. In another study, everyone who received healing in a laboratory test had increased DHEAS hormone levels. Pharmaceuticals will never do expensive blind studies on energy healing because there is no profit in a gift of nature we can all harness for free. Healing energy is real energy, not imagined. When I ask God to send healing, my hands heat up and vibrate and the energy never fails to come. As long as humans have existed, healing has been with us—but it is mostly hidden and only hinted at by the Spiritual Masters. Christ, a healer, was more vocal than most and told His followers to practice doing healing. Bill received surgery and radiation. I chose to only have surgery. We both had healing. My cancer was "Stage 2" and he was told he had "fast-growing prostate cancer." Oncologists expected us to be dead by now. Which saved us? Healing energy, traditional medicine or both?

I have been on a spiritual journey since I was sixteen, recovering from abusive religious teachings—the misrepresentation of God. I was taught we were here to suffer, and I sabotaged my own happiness until I changed my beliefs. During my journey, I was guided to people with spiritual gifts: teachers, healers and psychics who helped me survive. Of course, you don't give your master your MasterCard. Most con artists aren't possessed by the devil, but their greed and ego get in the way. Sure, there are "false prophets," some in church. The skeptics find one fraud and conclude every healer is one. They believe healing only happened in the distant past. The truth is, miraculous healing occurs every day all over the world, but you won't hear about it in most doctors' offices, although any experienced physician probably has witnessed a miracle.

Fifty years ago, I was rescued by angels. My hope is this true story will finally reach those it will heal and prevent someone else from ending their own life.

Always love,

Diana

Chapter 2

Buns and Rosaries

Dear Penny,

Bill and I went to Peterson's Shoes today, in downtown Anoka. When Bill was in grade school and his family lived farther north in Forest Lake, his parents brought the kids to Peterson's to buy Buster Brown shoes. I remembered you bought your last pair of shoes there. The chemotherapy and resulting congestive heart failure had caused your feet to swell and get numb with neuropathy. Before your last trip, you bought bigger shoes at Peterson's. I'm writing again, Penny. It's going to take me a while because my wrists hurt and my hands get numb from doing transcription, so I have to pace myself when doing any extra keyboarding. I'll get there. I promise.

Dad in orchestra with French horn and bass fiddle

In 1947, Mom and Dad had three little boys, aged six, four and three. Mom was a devout Catholic who believed sex was designed by God to create children—not for fun. Dad was working two jobs. He managed an advertising department at 3M Company and played French horn and bass fiddle in a "big band" three nights a week. Mom, named Adelaide—Addie for short—wanted to have a girl, but her doctor advised her not to get pregnant again because she had benign tumors in her uterus that might rupture and she could bleed to death. But Dad got "lucky" one more time, and Mom got pregnant. She gained less than ten pounds with her pregnancy. She went into labor six weeks early and was told at the hospital they could hear no fetal heartbeat and she would have a stillbirth. This was before ultrasounds. When her three-pound, one-ounce baby girl was delivered, Mom bled profusely. She went into toxic shock; her eyes rolled back in her head. They were expecting the afterbirth and I popped out: four pounds, two ounces—doomed to be the fat one. Mom had premature twin girls, both alive. Her blood pressure was dangerously high. My sister Donna and I were rushed to incubators.

Mom, hands full with twin girls and three boys

Next to us was another premature baby girl who would miraculously show up in my life forty years later.

Mom needed a hysterectomy, but the doctors convinced her to try a new treatment to atrophy her uterus with radiation. This was before federal safety regulations. Mom was microwaved. Her endocrine system and thyroid didn't work anymore. She was sick the rest of her life and became addicted to prescription drugs. The top of her bookcase bed was filled with medications, vitamins and supplements. Mom had worked as an RN before she had children and ordered whatever pills she wanted out of the PDR (Physician's Desk Reference), the legal drug catalog. Her family practice doctor, feeling guilty for the botched experimental radiation, prescribed whatever she wanted.

Eventually, Mom became a recluse. On uppers, she was a cleanliness fanatic, running the vacuum over our feet in frenzy or whacking us with a dust rag. On downers, she was in a three-day stupor, and we took turns checking her bed to be sure she was still alive. Dad had moved out of their bedroom and in with the boys.

She raised five children but seldom left the house. Unfortunately, Mom took the Catholic religion literally, believing that suffering was the way to earn heaven. If you weren't suffering you weren't serving God. They say the Catholic teachings have been relaxed, but in those days it was absolute. She sent us to a Catholic school where the nuns were very strict and the principal, Sister Agatha—we called her Sister Crabetha—was abusive. I was scared of committing a mortal sin—the worst kind—losing my soul and being sent to Hell. I had overheard my mother tell my aunt that my sister and I were her "cross to bear" because our birth was what destroyed her health. At age six I had my first survivor's guilt.

Our family in the early nineteen-fifties

I was taught we were born to suffer—that God wanted us to feel pain and offer it up to Heaven like a savings account. The more you suffered, the bigger your assets grew. How dare I have fun or be happy when my mother was up in the bedroom dying because I'd been born. I was doomed to attract suffering and became really good at it. Members of the church taught that our religion was the only true religion. They enjoyed believing, "I'm saved, and you're not." It was a smart way to keep you Catholic. The second worst thing I was taught by the nuns was that sex was evil; that I was my body and my body was dirty.

I was born with naturally curly hair, the opposite of my sister. This was before hair products like gel and mousse. It was a mass of blonde frizz that I put a rubber band around and pulled up into a ponytail. When it rained, it expanded. Sister Crabetha called me into her office and asked me how much time I spent on my hair. She scolded me, saying it was a sin of vanity to have curly hair. I later learned that Father Relic, the parish priest, was a close friend of my mother's; Sister

Crabetha didn't like it.

I looked up to my oldest brother David. I did everything he told me. He advised me to eat burnt toast because the charred bread would give me a great singing voice. Every morning for weeks I put my sliced bread down in the toaster four times on high until the kitchen was filled with smoke so I could be a rock star. It didn't work.

We lived in a big house on York Avenue and had lots of friends in the neighborhood. Mary and Judy were our very best buddies. We walked three miles to school together. In the summer we bicycled, swam and played hopscotch, jump rope, tag and softball. In the winter we sledded, skated and tobogganed. Although I was afraid of sinning, I had a lot of fun playing with my sister and our girlfriends. I tried to fit in but I felt different because I had a secret.

House we grew up in Saint Paul, Minnesota

When I was about six, my three brothers used to gang up on me and tickle me until I could hardly breathe. I kicked, fought and giggled until I wet my pants. When I was six and my brother David was about twelve he snuck into my bed, tickled me, pulled down my clown pajamas and thrust his finger inside me. It hurt. I didn't understand what he did or why. I don't remember it happening more than once. When I came downstairs for breakfast the next day I was sad and afraid. The physical pain was fleeting, but I believed "touching down there" was a sin, increasing the shame. It was the first time I wanted to leave my body and go home to Heaven. A child's soul, like the dying, is closer to God.

I loved my brother and heard my mom threaten to get the "switch" when she caught him touching himself, so I didn't dare tell her or anyone what happened. In fact, I didn't even remember it until years later when I had the first benign breast lump and a psychic told me it was a forgiveness issue. The lump manifested when my brother David died suddenly of a massive heart attack at age forty-seven. I worked out the grief with a counselor. I had hoped he would apologize, but I realized then that he was young too and as screwed up as I was. He went into the Christian Brotherhood. David has near-genius intelligence and excelled at everything he did. He became a classical guitarist and music teacher. Eventually he had a child with his girlfriend, but our family didn't know about his son until he was six years old because in the 1950s the church condemned children born out of marriage and David knew my mom couldn't handle it.

A big part of the Catholic ritual was confessing your sins to the priest. You could not go to communion at Sunday Mass and receive the host, a blessed small wafer of bread, unless you had knelt before the priest in the confessional. In church there was a small booth with a curtain and a screen between you and the pastor. After you told him your sins, he gave you a punishment called penance—usually a group of prayers to say—then your sins were forgiven and he made the sign of the cross in absolution. I remember when I was around eight years old I played church on the steps with my friends. I was the priest. I used my mom's wine goblet for the chalice and Necco wafers for the communion. I mimicked Latin, waving my hand over the candy and chanting what the priest's words sounded like to me: "Nabisco, Nabisco, Nabisco . . ." When my mom saw us, she pulled me into the house by my sweat-shirt and said I had committed the sin of blasphemy. "Women can never be priests!"

In every Mass before communion we beat our left breast and repeated three times, "I am not worthy, I am not worthy, I am not worthy." Is it a coincidence that is where the cancer grew? At home we had a prayer kneeler upstairs in the hallway where we were sent to pray when we were bad. There were statues of Mary and Jesus on the shelf above the kneeler at eye level, reminding us whom we were to emulate.

I remember when I received Holy Communion I wondered why I didn't feel bliss, since I was told the wafer had been changed to Christ's body and blood. I felt guilty the wafer stuck to the roof of my mouth like peanut butter and I had to use my finger to get it down. I'd been taught it was a sin to touch the holy bread.

When I was twelve, I quit going to confession with Father Relic because I believed he would recognize my voice and know my sins. That year, around Christmas time, Father Relic and his younger assistant priest came to our house to visit. He mentioned they had drunk a bit too much wine on their visits, and I could smell alcohol on their breath. They came into the living room. When I walked by to go into the kitchen, Father Relic grabbed my butt. I hurriedly walked down into the basement. I sat in the corner by the washer, confused and upset, and waited for the priests to leave. The hands that held the communion host in a holy sacrament grabbed my ass. I'd learned anything sexual out of marriage was a sin, but there was a more insidious message: girls had something men wanted. I didn't get it. Christ taught that we were not our body but our soul. The priest was supposed to be the example of Christ. I hated Father Relic, but I could not express my anger because I was taught that anger was a sin, especially for girls. Instead of standing up for myself, I swallowed my anger. The word "no" was not in my vocabulary. The sin of the impurity of thoughts about the body had been so distorted that students had their mouths washed out with soap for saying fart and girls were told never to wear shiny patent leather shoes because their underwear would reflect in them, tempting the evil lust of boys.

In grade school I memorized my Catechism, a series of religious questions and answers, and I never forgot the answer to why we were born: "to suffer in this world and be happy with God in the next." I felt guilty when I was happy.

The wonderful thing I learned in Catholicism was that Jesus was a healer who taught His followers to heal others. We studied the lives of saints who summoned miracles. Women were not allowed to be priests in the Church, but they could be healers and saints. I learned about miraculous physical healing performed by His followers who were fishermen, laborers and housewives. Perhaps this was the seed that led me to become a healer. But my excitement about healing was short lived. I prayed continually for my mother to get well and she didn't. It took me years to realize that as long as she believed sickness was her ticket to heaven she would not get well despite all my prayers.

There was one nun I loved who treated me gently. When I was nine Sister Francis Cabrini, named after the saint who had once visited the convent where the sisters lived, nominated me to lead the May procession and place the crown of roses on the statue of Mary. My name was randomly drawn out of a hat. I overheard other girls complaining that I won, saying, "She's not pretty enough"; "She doesn't deserve it"; "She got it because Father Relic likes her mother."

My mother was too sick to come to the May Procession. My dad was too busy to get away. I wore an ugly blue skirt printed with baskets of flowers on it and an itchy tulle underskirt, a white uniform blouse and the long, lace white veil I had worn for my holy communion. It had a tall, wavy crown shaped like a triceratops' head. All females had to wear something on their heads in church, a rule passed down from the church teaching that women were filthy because they menstruated.

I led the entire class from school to church that morning. Sister Cabrini took my hand, leading me into the nun's kitchen where we were normally not allowed. I slowly walked across the black-and-white checked linoleum to the large, industrial, steel refrigerator. She opened the double doors. Inside, next to a large block of yellow cheese, was a crown of tiny pink tea roses. Sister placed it on a purple velvet pillow for me to carry in the procession to place on the head of the giant statue of Mary that had been moved onto the altar for the celebration. The statue was ten feet tall with Mary wearing her traditional blue dress and veil. Her arms and hands were stretched open in welcome. Her feet stood on a serpent, crushing the open-mouthed snake that represented Satan.

The students sang hymns as I walked up the church steps and down the aisle to the altar. When I climbed on the ladder balancing the crown on the pillow, I slipped, hearing a communal sigh of sympathy as I caught my balance. As they sang the words ". . . we haste to crown thee now . . ." too low to reach her head, I tossed the crown up and it fell down over her nose. I could hear giggling as I leaned over and precariously reached to adjust the crown. Relieved it was in place, I hurried down to my seat in the front row next to the nuns.

One Saturday I was invited with three other girls to visit Sister Cabrini at the convent downtown on Exchange Street. At the time, I thought about becoming a nun. The nuns lived secluded in a narrow room with a small bed and dresser. They had a communal kitchen in the basement and a lounge with a fireplace near the entrance where they played cards and talked when it was allowed. The sisters took a vow of silence and spent many hours in mandatory isolation. To a gabby little girl, that was the most appalling vow of all.

The bathrooms had stalls like in school except for a separate tub room. The historical brick building was cold and institutional. I had no way of knowing someday I would move into that building on Exchange Street.

I loved the stories of the saints, miracles and healing I learned about at school but the example of Sister Crabetha was not so Christ-like. One winter day when you could see your breath turn to mist in the biting cold, I was outside playing at recess. I could hear Sister Crabetha ringing her heavy brass bell, signaling that playtime was over and it was time to go back into school. I followed in the long line moving toward the double doors, hearing the continuous ringing. Suddenly a small black puppy scampered around the corner of the school toward the open doors where it was warm. He sniffed the ground, searching for the scent of his owner, his ears flopping up and down. Sister Crabetha screamed, "Scat; get out. Out!" As the dog reached the door, she slammed the bell against the puppy's head. Blood spurted from his ear. He whimpered and fell off the concrete, landing onto the frozen ground. He was panting hard and looked scared. I wanted to run down and comfort him, but the nun yelled at us to "Get inside!"

Later, word spread in whispers through the school that the puppy died. The fourth grade class watched out the window when the grounds caretaker removed the dog. When my sister and I left Blessed Sacrament School that day, we were haunted by the blood-stained snow.

Always love,

Diana

Chapter 3

Saved by the Jell-O

Dear Penny,

Bill and I went to your favorite place for dessert on Main Street, Truffles and Torts, and had lunch. The mushroom soup was wonderful but the pumpkin cheesecake we shared was better. It had a tiny little marzipan pumpkin on top with a clove stem. So cute. I know you loved the old brick walls, the tin ceiling and the mouthwatering pastries and chocolates displayed behind the glass case. I believe you flit in and out from Heaven to earth watching us. Do you just eat light in Heaven? Your name, Penny, fit with your copper color, short hair and your shiny personality. The last year, when you were on experimental chemotherapy and lost your hair, your wig looked just like your real hair. You always looked sharp and no one who didn't know what you were going through would have known you were so sick. Back to my story. What got me so down?

At age fifteen, I was transferred to public school. My father could no longer afford a Catholic education for his girls. Everything was different. No one valued chastity and obedience but instead valued clothes and boys in that order—two things I knew nothing about after wearing a school uniform and a having fashion-less mother whose wardrobe consisted of flannel nightgowns and jelly-stained robes.

My mother had a closet filled with cocktail dresses and jewelry that hinted at another life before she had children. Donna and I liked playing dress up in her closet. I loved prancing around in Mom's short fur coat, like a movie star. I was taught never to waste, so having the bigger breasts I did not get a new bra when I developed but was handed down my mother's elastic, yellowed old bra with ten hooks. I also still wore a Catholic scapula around my neck: two flat strings with two postage-stamp-sized materials imprinted with figures of Saint Christopher and Saint Francis. It was blessed by the bishop and I was told never to take it off, so I wore it in the bathtub until the saints were worn off, leaving two little rags hanging from the strings. On the first day of middle school, I innocently went to gym class wearing the monster bra and the scapula. As I walked into the locker room, girls were undressing in front of one another. I was mortified as I turned around the old elastic bra to unhook it and my breasts flopped out in front of everyone. Then the gym teacher made me remove my sacred scapula before entering the swimming pool. By the time my first gym class was over, my scapula and my last shred of self-esteem were gone.

A girl named Sheila strutted confidently, showing off her huge breasts and narrow waist. When my stare reached her face I realized we had been classmates at Blessed Sacrament. We were opposites drawn to each other by the scars of Sister Crabetha. Sheila liked to be in control and I was obedient, so we got along.

I had to be careful around boys who were "after one thing: sex." I'd been taught that it was better to let a man kill you than to lose your virginity, a mortal sin punished with eternal Hell for girls only. Boys who had sex were admired as "studs," but girls were labeled "sluts." Mother told me stories of saints who were slaughtered to save their virginity. They were heroines. My mother's favorite was Saint Lucy, who had beautiful eyes and plucked her own eyes out to stop a suitor from pursuing her! Mom convinced me to take Saint Lucy for my confirmation name, but I really wanted St. Rose, a holy nun. She wore a crown of rose thorns pushed into her head to mimic the crown of thorns Jesus was forced to wear at the crucifixion. St. Rose was often depicted in a rose garden with blood dripping down her face, my favorite holy card. I collected cards with pictures of saints the way my brothers collected baseball cards.

At fifteen I had a crush on a boy named Stan, who was in my journalism class. He was the class clown. Because he talked to me, I thought he liked me. I hadn't noticed he talked to everyone. The teacher often told him to be quiet. I saved money from a babysitting job to buy Stan a silver bracelet with his name engraved on it. Stan was out of school for an entire week in late April. He seldom missed school, especially Wednesdays when he had a deadline for his sports column in the school paper. Sheila convinced me to call Stan and find out what was wrong. On Friday night, my hands shaking, I dialed Stan. He answered the phone and told me he'd missed school because his grandmother died. We talked for over an hour, and he asked me to meet him at 11:00 p.m. at his house. His parents were in Illinois settling her estate. I could give him his bracelet.

I wrapped his gift in blue tissue paper tied with a purple bow. I wore a soft blue sweater and jeans with my new white ski jacket. The temperature outside was only thirty degrees. It was snowing lightly. I quietly shut the front door and crept down the front steps. He lived about six blocks from my house. As I walked through the dark, empty streets, the wind boxed my face. I pulled my hood up over my ears. There were hard, crusty mounds of old, dirty snow on the boulevard left from a hard winter. As I walked up the driveway, Stan came out of the back door. He was not wearing a jacket and stomped his tennis shoes against the pavement, trying to warm his feet. He grabbed my arm and steered me to the garage. "Want to see my new motorcycle?"

"Sure," I agreed, following him. He manually opened the creaky door and turned on a single lightbulb hanging by a black cord over a small, worn workbench. The cracked concrete floor was stained with oil. Stan took me over to the metallic-gold Electroglyde and told me to sit down on the smooth, black leather seat. I reluctantly lifted my leg over the chrome fender and sat down. When I stood up to get off, the heavy bike started to fall sideways. Stan ran over to catch it, swearing, "Fuck, drop my bike and you're dead." Caught off guard, I stepped back, alarmed by his easy cussing.

He went over and opened the passenger door of his mom's car. "Sit down," he said, walking to the driver's side. I got in and handed him the package. "What's this?"

"It's for your birthday," I mumbled. He opened the box

and put on the silver bracelet.

"Cool," he said. "I like it." And he scooted closer on the bench seat, kissing me on the cheek. I turned away, looking out the car window at the cement floor. It was not a romantic place for a first kiss. His hand brushed my thigh as he moved closer. He pulled my jacket off my lap and gripped my left breast.

"Stop it. You're hurting me!" I pulled down on the door handle. "I have to go before my dad knows I'm gone." Before I could get the door open, Stan pulled me back, kissed me hard on the lips and tried to shove his tongue in my mouth. I froze. He reached around me, opened the glove compartment, took something out and switched on the radio. The lyrics from a popular love song filled the car saying if you break my heart, you will never get to Heaven. Before I could make another move, Stan switched open a razor knife and held it up, threatening, "Just do what I say." While I obediently took my pants down, I silently recited the holy names, "Jesus, Mary and Joseph; Jesus, Mary and Joseph . . . Jesus, Mary and Joseph . . . Help me."

As I waited for the saints to arrive, Stan, angry that I wasn't participating, violently raped me, swearing at his difficulty, "Are you a fucking virgin?" Then he was done and it was over. I felt a surge of pain and saw the knife sitting on the floor of the car on top of the gift wrapping. Stan hurriedly dressed himself and mumbled, "Don't tell anyone."

I ignored him as I pulled on my clothes and coat, thinking how I should have fought or let him kill me. I'd have gone straight to Heaven as a martyr and pleased my mother. It was a lonely walk home in the dark. I almost took a detour to the woods near our house, wanting to take an overdose of my mother's barbiturates and fall asleep down by the creek. The snow would blanket my body, and I'd fertilize the wild violets in the spring. I went home and took a bath, thinking of pulling my head under the warm, sudsy water, when my sister knocked on the door of the bathroom asking if I was almost done. Like a wet puppy I dragged myself out, wrapped a towel around my body and went to bed, falling asleep before my hair was dry. I didn't tell Donna or my mother. I didn't tell

Sheila or my teachers. I didn't tell anyone.

I stayed home for the next four days, depressed and afraid I might be pregnant. I could not face seeing Stan again. When I got back to school I begged the student advisor to get me out of the journalism class I loved. I changed my route to class in order to avoid Stan. Then I heard some boys walking in back of me smacking their lips, taunting, "Hey, can I get me some? Stan says you give out." They walked by, snickering.

I went home and wrote in my journal. Writing my feelings was keeping me alive. I always stayed up late and watched *The Steve Allen Show*. He was a Hollywood icon who started the Tonight Show, a comedian who made me laugh. I asked my dad to buy me his autobiography, *Mark It and Strike It*, but it was out of print. My father said he would try to find a copy at an old bookstore downtown. So I decided to live a little longer. I had something to look forward to. Every day I decided whether to live or to kill myself.

Sheila and I became close friends. Almost weekly we went on a liquid diet to lose weight and by the end of the week we quit and binged on Cheetos and ice cream. We loved reading teen magazines about Hollywood stars and roller skating on Friday nights. Sheila liked to get me in trouble.

One sunny morning in late May, I was home from school sick with asthma. I had taken my medication, ephedrine sulfate, that made me nervous and shaky. Sheila skipped school and called me. She assumed I was faking because she always was. Sheila was never sick. She persuaded me to bike over to her house and get into her dad's liquor cabinet. I had never tasted alcohol. We hated the taste of the whisky, so we opened two beer bottles and poured out half the bottle and added whisky, vodka and rum. I had no idea alcohol was dangerous, especially mixed with prescription drugs. Sheila wanted to run away and ride our bikes from Minnesota to California. All I wanted to do was stop feeling.

We plugged our noses and chugged the awful concoction. At first I didn't notice anything, but soon a hot fireball exploded in my belly and I felt a tingle in my forehead. We stacked records on the phonograph turntable and danced around the living room to the Supremes, the Beatles and the Beach Boys.

Sheila's Chihuahua ran around us, barking, and then retreated under the sofa, then darted back out, chasing us again. Together we fell on the blue carpet, laughing. We went into her parents' bedroom, found her dad's condoms and blew them up, sending them flying through the air making a farting sound on their way to the floor. We couldn't walk straight. Around 1:00 p.m. we realized that Sheila's mother would be home soon so we got on our royal blue bikes and rode a long way, dangerously swerving in and out of traffic. I had forgotten my glasses at Sheila's house and everything was a blur. We got about a mile down Maryland Avenue when the light at the intersection of Arcade changed to red. Sheila zoomed across the street. Nauseated and dizzy, I could not maneuver the bike around a parked car. I passed out and tipped over onto the sidewalk. When I came to, there were people standing around me. With only a view of their shoes, I heard a voice from a pair of red high heels: "She's drunk. I called the police."

The next thing I knew, I was lifted into the backseat of a patrol car. Sheila was on the other side. We were taken to the police station. A reporter took our photo. Sheila was throwing up in the wastepaper can while I tried to hide under a bench. He couldn't use the picture because we were minors, but we did make the local evening news and the St. Paul Pioneer Press newspaper: *Girls Arrested for B.W.I—Biking While Intoxicated.*

That evening we were taken to a detention center. My dad and sister visited us. He said when the police called he told them they had the wrong person; it could not be his obedient daughter. Hungover, I felt sick and cried myself to sleep in the locked cell. The next morning my dad picked me up to appear in court. He didn't bring me clean clothes. I was still wearing blue jeans and a dirty sweatshirt with my frizzy hair sticking out like an abandoned bird's nest. Dressed in a proper pink dress, Sheila came in with her parents and their attorney. Her parents were given a lecture about having liquor available to minors. In private, her lawyer got her off, and I was given a year's probation. For a whole year I had to report weekly to a probation officer who was stern and indifferent.

One weeknight I was contemplating doing myself in again. Everyone in the house was in bed but I couldn't sleep. I went downstairs and turned on the television. Steve Allen was on. I had a full bottle of painkillers I had taken from my mother's bookcase headboard. I took a Fred Flintstone jelly glass out of the cupboard, filled it with water and went back to sit in Dad's recliner. I took three pills quickly, gagging, and swallowed more water to get them down. I turned to watch the show and Steve was climbing up a ladder to the diving board over a swimming pool filled with Jell-O. He signaled the bandleader for a drumroll and jumped in. I waited impatiently for him to pop back out with gelatin and whipped cream dripping from his trademark black glasses. I laughed and became hypnotized by the television show. When the next commercial came on, I thought, ". . . There was something I was going to do. Oh, yeah, kill myself," but I was too tired. I screwed the cap back on the bottle, put it in my robe, drank my water and went up to bed. It was a good thing I didn't die that night. The next day my dad brought me a surprise gift.

"I found that autobiography of Steve Allen you wanted!" Thrilled, I ran up to my bedroom and began to read. It was a Friday night. I read all weekend. It was odd that a sixteen year old had a crush on a man in his forties, but something magical happened. I learned that this famous Hollywood Icon was raised Catholic. He was born the day after Christmas and named after Saint Stephen, who was stoned to death. His book was dedicated to "Sister Seraphia who had a sense of humor." This man who saved my life by making me laugh had written about exactly what was bothering me—the contradictions of religion. He too was taught modesty and was ashamed to undress in gym class. I felt less alone. Then I discovered he also had asthma as a kid, like me. On page 242 was an eleven-page poem Steve Allen had written in 1938 when he was a seventeen year old attending Hyde Park High in Chicago. A troubled teenage boy's words reached twenty-six years ahead into the heart of a suicidal girl in St. Paul, Minnesota. He felt the despair I felt and not only survived but became a famous television entertainer, a comedian, a talented pianist and an author who wrote fifty-four books. When I closed the last page, I understood the power of words. I wanted to become an author and help someone feel less alone the way Steve Allen had for me. That night I wrote him a long, long letter telling him how he stopped me from taking that overdose. I remember asking my dad for a stamp. As I left the house to mail my letter, he said, "He gets thousands of letters a week. His secretary probably answers them. Don't get your hopes up." He didn't know how much I needed to get my hopes up. I'm sure the angels walked down the block with me to the corner mailbox that morning.

A few months later I had a really bad day at school. I had been asked by my art teacher to help design the backdrop for the school musical, *Oklahoma*. I didn't feel confident and Stan was going to be in the play, so I was concerned about how I would avoid him. The dark thoughts of suicide were back. I was busy doing babysitting for a neighbor after school three nights a week.

One day after school I took the mail out of the box and set it on Dad's desk. It was usually all addressed to him. Then I remembered I was waiting for a teen magazine in the mail. I shuffled through the pile and glimpsed a return address from Hollywood. My heartbeat sped up when I pulled out the letter from Steve Allen:

December 28, 1964
Dear Diana:

Thank you for your kind letter of December 8th.

You might be interested to know that my first reaction when you asked me to tell you about the meaning of life was to make a note to send you my autobiography—and then a paragraph later in your letter I discovered you had already read it.

Under separate cover I am sending you some of my other books. I don't really know how much they will teach you about life, but I hope at the very least they will suggest to you that it is well worth living.

I doubt if there is a person alive who has not asked himself at one time or another whether life is really worth living.

Therefore, you need not feel that you are unusual in that respect. Almost everyone, however, does conclude that life is indeed precious.

Write me another letter a few months from now and let me know how you are getting along and whether any of the ideas in the literature I am sending to you turned out to be helpful.

> All good wishes, cordially,
> Steve Allen

I was thrilled and that night when I turned on *The Steve Allen Show* I got chills. In the sixties there were only a few television channels and he was the hottest celebrity on TV. He wrote me back! It was the beginning of a lifetime of correspondence. I would eventually meet Steve Allen, make him laugh, visit his home and become close to his beloved wife Jayne. Receiving Steve Allen's letter was the first time I felt my desire went out to the Universe and the Universe answered.

Always love,

Diana

Chapter 4

A Cold Draft

Dear Penny,

This weekend Bill and I went for a walk at the Coon Rapids Dam Park and walked the trail along the Mississippi River where the canopy of trees casts shadows along the path. Like life, where there is sun there are shadows. It's a dual reality.

By age seventeen, I'd dodged the suicide bullet temporarily but almost died from an asthma attack. Being a teenager was intense enough with the flood of hormones rushing through me, but my asthma medications made me even more wired. When my bronchial tubes began to close off my airway I couldn't catch my breath. The little red prescription pills of ephedrine sulfate increased my heart rate, rushing more oxygen to open the airways. They also made me shaky, sleepless and anxious. While my mother was high on prescription Dexedrine—legal speed—I was frazzled on asthma meds. My mother sometimes gave my brother Dexies (Dexedrine)—popular uppers—in exchange for doing housework. In the sixties any woman who was tired could get some from her family doctor. When she couldn't sleep she could get some downers (barbiturates). There was no understanding of chemical dependency back then.

In August, Sheila and I went to the state fair. One of the performers in the grandstand was Fabian, a popular singer. I glued his name in glitter on a black velvet bow and wore it in my hair. His hit song was "Tiger Man," so I made him a cake shaped like a tiger. We tried to get backstage at the grandstand with the cake, but a security guard stopped us. I had tears in my eyes. Feeling pity on us, the guard took us through a backdoor and outside. We followed him to a trailer. Inside there was Fabian, wearing a three-piece brown suit, smoking a cigarette. He took the cake, kissed me on the cheek and gave me an autographed photo.

Sheila and I left the trailer giggling and went to the Midway to go on the rides and play games in the arcade. When we were done, Sheila—who loved horses—convinced me to go to the horse barn. I plugged my nose to block out the smell of manure. Within fifteen minutes I could not breathe. I was wheezing so badly that I had to stop every few feet to catch my breath. Sheila was petting a black horse when I whispered, "I have to get out of here." I hardly made it out the door and collapsed on an outdoor bench, gasping for air. A woman came over to me, recognizing an asthma attack, and offered to get help. There were no cell phones yet. She went over to two policemen on horseback. I saw her pointing at me. I used my asthma inhaler but it didn't help. My chest hurt. I felt light-headed like I might pass out. Sheila came out of the barn and saw me but went to buy a snow cone. She was licking her dessert, oblivious, when an ambulance stopped in front of the bench. "Someone must have fallen off a ride," she said, surprised when the emergency responders helped me into the ambulance. We were driven to the state fair emergency clinic. They took my vitals and hurried us back into the ambulance. The driver put on the siren and rushed us to Bethesda Hospital's emergency room where I was given a shot of adrenaline. I had immediate relief but was trembling from the medication. The doctor said, "You could have died. You must be allergic to animal dander." I hoped one day I would outgrow my asthma like my dad did. It was bad enough feeling like I was suffocating, then asthma inhalers became associated with nerds. I can see now that being sick with asthma eventually led me to find a healer and to become one.

After high school I went on a liquid diet and lost twenty pounds. I was beautiful for three weeks in 1967. I got rid of my glasses and bought contact lenses and dyed my dead-grass-colored hair light blonde, the color it was when I was a little girl. I enjoyed having boys look at me for the first time. I started college.

On my eighteenth birthday my twin Donna and her boyfriend set me up on a date with Michael. He had been in my tenth-grade English class, but we had never talked. I spent hours getting ready for my first date. I redid my makeup three times, tried to contour my cheeks with foundation and tried on five outfits, settling finally on a rose-red sweater and black pants. Dad answered the front door and let Michael in.

He had curly, dark hair and slate blue eyes and white, perfect teeth. A fading tan looked gold against the pale yellow of his shirt. He wore dark blue jeans, had a military posture and polished, black boots.

Michael took me to Matt and Gene's Pizza. I'd never eaten a restaurant pizza. Our family only made the kind that came in a box. Michael ordered a pepperoni sausage pizza with mushrooms and extra cheese and a pitcher of cold draft beer. We were underage, but he knew the manager well and nobody asked any questions. I'd never had alcohol except for the driving-bike-while-intoxicated incident, but I didn't say no when he poured me a glass of foamy beer. By the time the pizza came we were giggling. Michael lifted a piece off the warm pan. As he ate, the long strings of mozzarella hung from his full, shiny mouth, tempting me.

"You have nice lips," I said.

"You too," he reached across the booth and gave me a kiss.

I had one mug of beer. I didn't get sick, but I knew now what having a "buzz on" was.

We sat in the red vinyl booth and talked for a couple of hours. He looked sad when he told me he had recently put his dog to sleep. She had cancer. But Michael was looking forward to going to a breeder to get a golden retriever puppy for hunting. The waitress was cleaning off the tables hinting it was time to leave. I didn't want the night to end, to go back to the house. When we got home Michael walked me to the front door. Mother's bedroom window upstairs was open, and I could hear her singing a somber Gregorian chant. Mortified, I looked down at the damp autumn leaves that clung to Michael's boots. I was grateful he didn't mention it.

"Thanks; I had fun!" I said, looking down at the steps.

"Me, too." Michael zipped up his windbreaker. I grabbed on and held him, pressing my face against his chest. He held me for a few seconds and caressed my hair. I felt warmth stirring in my heart.

"When can I see you again?" he whispered.

"Come back in an hour," I said into his shirt, afraid to let go.

"I'll call you tomorrow." He turned to leave. He did call back and we became a couple. The Vietnam War was going on. Michael told me he was sure he would get a deferment because he had a pin in his leg from a car accident, but every night in the news we heard stories of young men who thought they were safe but were drafted and came home in body bags.

First love Michael and Diana 1967

I continued to log in my journal. *The Steve Allen Show* helped me forget my insecurities, and when I laughed the pain disappeared. I wrote Steve Allen again and he wrote back suggesting I do volunteer work and get counseling.

Taking his advice, I volunteered at what was then called a "hospital for crippled children," an ominous stone structure located on the grounds of Lake Phalen with gargoyles staring down from the corbels of the roof. As a candy striper, I had to wear a red-and-white pinafore over a starched white blouse, white stockings and thick, rubber-soled, orthopedic shoes. Unfortunately, visiting abandoned children that had become wards of the state was a horror I was not prepared for. There was a toddler deformed from the drug Thalidomide given to his mother when she was pregnant who had no arms and legs, only a body and a head.

I made friends with Jenny, a little girl with stumps for legs. She proudly showed me how her catheter worked, draining urine from her bladder into a bag on the side of her wheel-chair. I often stayed after my shift and played cards with her or wheeled her to the auditorium to watch kids' movies like *Shirley Temple* or *The Three Stooges*. That fall my asthma worsened and I began to miss some Saturdays. When I went back, Jenny hugged me tightly and asked me not to leave. "I want you to adopt me," she said. I was overwhelmed that this nine-year-old girl thought of me as a mother. I was eighteen but emotionally twelve. I told her I was an immature student who had no way to care for a little girl. She didn't understand. When I said goodbye at the end of the year she was devastated. Volunteering had only added to my guilt and confusion. How did unwanted children fit with a loving God? Maybe getting counseling, like Steve Allen suggested, would help.

Michael and I were falling in love. We often made out in his car at a spot near the railroad tracks called Big Sandy. We watched swallows that nested in the clay cliffs nearby swoop-ing through the air. I was afraid he would know I was raped and not a virgin and he was a good Catholic boy so we cud-dled and kissed with our clothes on. I turned on the radio, straddled him and rocked. We had orgasms without intercourse. My beloved Michael showed me I could love and be loved.

Always love,

Diana

Chapter 5

The Thorazine Shuffle

Dear Penny,

Last evening Bill and I met friends at Billy's in Anoka and sat outside in the enclosed patio. Years ago you and I met here for nachos and a margarita. For late September, it was still warm enough to just wear a jean jacket. The vines attached to the brick façade had turned crimson and gold. The sparrows nesting in the leaves chirped their evening song as the sun set around 7:30 p.m. We ate burgers, drank beer and shared the onion rings. We all had a toast to our angel, Penny, and savored the fresh air, knowing we'd soon be huddled inside for the winter. Some people move away from Minnesota because of the winters, but I think the cold makes us appreciate the seasons more.

Finally, after years of being shut down, someone bought, renovated and reopened Hans Bakery, famous for their pastry with custard filling called the "beehive." Now they have little serving-size ones called beestings. Bill brought me one today because I was having a stressful day at work with lots of stat dictations. He's very thoughtful but making me fat.

I was in culture shock in college. I'd never felt so alone. I'd been taught by my given religion unquestioning obedience and that as sinners we were not capable of making good decisions for ourselves. This led me to look up to everyone as an authority, not just the clergy. I never considered what I wanted but followed whatever I was advised. My inability to stand up for myself led to the following disaster that would change my life for decades to come. A professor advised me that it was a waste of time for a woman to get a degree. He said women were only in college to get a husband. He was an example of education having nothing to do with intelligence.

Writing had opened my mind but not my mouth. I was looking for a way out of the self-hatred religion had imprisoned me in just so I might survive. It was the sixties: the perfect time to go on a spiritual search and discover the difference between man-made, politically-oppressive religious dogma and spirituality, the experience of God in your life. I thought I was alone, but there was a mass consciousness rising. Seventy-eight million baby boomers were entering the Age of Aquarius, sweeping us to move out of the darkness.

I loved being with Michael, but I thought it would only last until he found out I was not a virgin. Sheila was engaged to be married and I was her maid of honor. She was attending beauty school to become a hairdresser. I agreed to have her practice on me and touch up the dark roots of my blonde hair.

Sheila applied the chemical dye and wrapped my hair in plastic. We visited while the color set. She didn't put on the timer. More than thirty minutes had gone by when she rinsed off the foam. When I saw a snicker on her face, I ran to look in the bathroom mirror. My entire head of hair, except for the inch of growth at the root, was army green.

I immediately called my dad to take me to a salon. They tried to cover it with a dark brown dye but nothing would cover the snot green. The beautician said I was lucky my hair hadn't fallen out. She told me that anyone in beauty school would have known not to mix the dye she did with the color I already had on my hair. How could I have trusted Sheila? I had wanted to wear my long blonde hair in puffy curls called love locks for her wedding. The hairdresser cut my hair to an inch long. I looked like a prisoner of war. I hid from Michael and would not answer his calls. I can't believe I was still the maid of honor in Sheila's wedding. She made sure I would not look better than she did. My emerging confidence dropped back to zero.

I decided to take Steve Allen's advice and get counseling. I was given a test that was written in the 1930s called the Minnesota Multiphasic Personality Inventory (MMPI). There were hundreds of questions, many about bathroom habits, asking the description of your turds.

Then I read the religious questions. Back then I didn't

know the term religiosity. But I see now with my belief in Spirit, I was in big trouble. In fact, when I now read the true/false questions listed below that were asked, I realize if Jesus took the MMPI he'd be labeled and put on Prozac:

- *I often feel a tight band around my head.*
- *I believe in a life hereafter.*
- *My mother is a good woman.*
- *I think I would like the work of a building contractor.*
- *I do not have a great fear of snakes.*
- *I believe I am being plotted against.*
- *My soul sometimes leaves my body.*
- *I would like to be a nurse.*
- *I have been inspired to a program of life based on duty, which I have since carefully followed.*
- *I have no fear of water.*
- *If I was in trouble with several friends who were as guilty as I was, I would rather take the whole blame than give them away.*
- *My thoughts these days turn more and more to death and the life hereafter.*

Jesus would be accused of having delusions of grandeur when he accepted dying for the sins of the world and be labeled codependent. I can see now that the test defined spiritual beliefs as hallucinations. Some therapists still have a prejudice against spirituality, calling any belief beyond the physical "magical thinking." Being a Virgin Mary wannabe, I didn't know my answers put me in danger.

After taking the test, I was told that I needed to be hospitalized for my own safety. I was taken to the locked psych ward and injected with heavy doses of Thorazine, an anti-psychotic drug that I was allergic to. Most people gained weight on the drug, but I lost seventeen pounds in two weeks and became dehydrated. I had severe loss of memory and blurred vision. I moved slowly, as though my feet were large stones, doing the Thorazine shuffle.

In lockup I met an entire counter culture my mother would never have approved of. The hospital was one of a few places in the world where sex change operations were being performed. I met Lee, a sweet and funny plus-sized drag queen with perfectly manicured nails. Part of his therapy was to dress as a woman preparing for his change. I was fascinated by a Cuban woman with long black hair and large green eyes. She wore heavy makeup, false eyelashes and dressed in a plunging neckline that exposed her implanted melon breasts. Rumor was she was a stripper. One night two policemen visited her. A girl named Linda frightened me the most, dragging her mobile IV unit across the ward. She was a severe anorexic/bulimic and smelled from the state of ketosis. She was 5'7" and weighed seventy-five pounds. Her starving body was consuming itself, eating the muscle of her vital organs. In those days anyone considered different was thrown in lockup: chemically dependent, delusional, mentally deficient, blind, too skinny, too fat, depressed, epileptic, etc. These souls were my dear friends. The healing I received was from my fellow inmates.

As part of occupational therapy, I was asked to help do some back-up filing in the medical records department. There I discovered old psychiatric records using terms to label patients as "feeble-minded, idiot, moron and imbecile."

My roommate had hysterical paralysis. She had wanted to be a nun and had also been taught that touching was bad. Someone had held her hand and it folded shut and was paralyzed. She had hypnotherapy that worked. We celebrated with a Dr. Pepper from the vending machine the day her hand began to open like a butterfly emerging from its cocoon. My assigned psychiatrist was not so progressive. When my dad's insurance money ran out, I was sent to live in the basement of a nursing home to work for room and board. I lived in a barracks-like room with five other women that society had discarded.

The first night I saw a young girl maneuvering her wheelchair into the lounge to watch television. It was Jenny from the children's hospital I had volunteered at. She didn't recognize me then, thinner with short brown hair. It was an eerie synchronicity. We did eventually play cards together, but we never mentioned the hospital.

I worked an eight-hour shift, changing diapers and bathing residents in exchange for three meals a day and a thin cot in a cold room shared with the others. There was a girl with Down Syndrome who wore thick glasses, a paraplegic, two "mentally ill" women so drugged up I didn't know what was wrong with them and a tiny woman four feet tall with a club foot. Her alarm woke me in the morning. I heard her dragging her leg as she walked to her job in the laundry at 6:00 a.m. Luckily the nurses did not monitor my medications. I was able to slowly wean myself off of the Thorazine. I hid the pills in the elastic side pocket of my suitcase, becoming more lucid with each day. The angels were working overtime again. Sometimes I am not able to hear their whispers, but I know I was guided one day to hear a nurse's conversation.

Six weeks after I'd arrived, I was sitting in a high-back chair in the lounge near the front desk and overheard one of the nurses on the phone say, "Diana is the first schizophrenic we've had." Oh my God; I had to escape or I might never have gotten out, so I made plans.

I loved an elderly woman named Myrtle. She lived in half of a shared room behind a curtain but was grateful to have a window. Myrtle was fragile and when I finished giving her a backrub her tremoring hand pulled a lemon shortbread cookie from a cellophane package, insisting I take it. Her weathered hands were speckled with brown spots and raised veins that looked like earthworms—the way mine look now.

One morning as I ran her bath water I saw a hearse pull up outside the nursing home. When I got to Myrtle's room, the bed had already been stripped and she was gone. I was trembling. This was the day I would escape. I called and asked my father to come and get me against medical advice. I was out in the suburbs, and he could not come until after work. When I finished my shift, I ate a bowl of leftover tuna casserole in the kitchen, took the elevator down to the basement, grabbed my packed suitcase and walked out the back delivery door to the driveway. Thank God my dad was waiting in his green station wagon. As he drove away, I said a prayer for Jenny and the residents who might never leave.

I was back to abnormal. That misdiagnosis haunted me for years to come. I eventually learned the father of psychology,

"Sigmoid Freud," told survivors of incest that they enjoyed being raped by their fathers and "wanted it." The misogynist who coined the phrase *penis envy* was addicted to opium and died of cancer of the mouth, a psychosomatic illness caused by vagina envy. His goatee beard mimicked the female escutcheon (muff).

If I had listened to the so-called experts and not listened to my body's toxic reaction and my intuition, I might still be in the basement of that nursing home.

Always love,

Diana

Chapter 6

Get Back Down There

Dear Penny,

I have felt your presence around me lately. Bill is getting arthritis, has bad knees with one replacement and is planning on retiring next year. I'd love to retire and do more healing work and writing. Hopefully not too long from now. I'm writing on my laptop in bed and Bill is sleeping next to me. I don't like it when it gets dark early and we have less light.

Well, after my escape from the nut hatchery, Michael came back to me. He didn't care that my hair was cut short. You're probably wondering how I was mentally. I was oversensitive, my emotions ran hot and cold—never tepid—and I still felt like it was me against the world. Paranoid schizophrenia or as Dr. Garvey, a psychiatrist I worked for, wisely put it, "the definition of a teenager."

I got a nurse's aide job at St. John's Hospital, working in the newborn nursery. After the babies were delivered I washed, weighed and measured them. I rolled their tiny feet on ink-pads and stamped their footprints on their birth certificates. I changed diapers and bottle-fed newborns. I loved the babies. They were so soft, perfect and innocent. That job was the most positive experience I'd had since I was a little girl chosen to crown the statue of Mary at the May procession. I kept my journal and wrote poetry, but I was afraid the staff would learn I was crazy and fire me. I stopped questioning life and concentrated on loving Michael, dreaming of marriage and having my own baby. After we reunited, I wanted to make love to Michael but was afraid he could tell I wasn't a virgin.

One weekend in early spring, Michael's dad and sisters were out of town visiting relatives. That Friday night we went for a pizza and our usual pitcher of beer and back to his house.

I sat on the sofa while Michael went into the kitchen to get a bottle of wine. After a noisy search through the drawer for a corkscrew, he reappeared with red wine and two crystal wine glasses. He poured slowly. In a toast he touched the rim of his glass to mine: "to our love." When they were empty we were lying next to each on the sofa.

I kissed his eyelids. I gently touched his hair, his lips, his face. He darted his tongue in my mouth, sending a suggestive signal through me. Michael gently unhooked my bra and cupped my breasts in his warm hands. We silently lifted ourselves off the sofa and hand-in-hand walked upstairs to his bedroom. My heart beat quickly with some trepidation, but Michael was slow and gentle. "I don't want this to ever end," he whispered.

"I know, Michael; I love you so." I snuggled up to him and suddenly overcome with emotion began to sob.

"What's the matter? Did I hurt you?" Michael caressed my hair.

"No, it's not you. I . . . I . . . have tell you. I was raped when I was sixteen. He had a knife. I'm sorry!" I got out of bed and put my clothes on.

"Who was it? I'll beat the crap out of him."

"I'm not telling you that. I went to meet him. I didn't tell anyone."

"You didn't even tell your mother?"

"I should have let him kill me. I'd have gone straight to heaven as a martyr and pleased my mother." I bent over, to put on my socks and tennis shoes, when Michael pulled me back on the bed.

"Stop it! That's the past. It doesn't change my feelings. Besides, that's bullshit. You can't believe everything you were told by the nuns. You sound like my dad. He won't get married again because he's a divorced Catholic." I was incredulous Michael hadn't swallowed everything like I did. "I don't think a nun or priest who has never had sex should be judging us." Michael took my hand reassuringly. "Come on. We have our whole lives ahead of us."

The next few months I was so happy. I loved my job. I loved Michael. I knew we would get married and I would escape from my mother. A few weeks later, Michael called me from the train depot in downtown St. Paul. "I can't talk long. I was drafted. I'm on my way to boot camp."

"No. You told me you were getting a deferment! Don't go. Please, don't go."

"Diana, I have to go. I won't be able to write for a while."

"Please, Michael. You're all I have."

"I have to go. I love you." He hung up. He was gone.

I went down on the kitchen floor still holding onto the cord phone and cried hysterically. "Please, God, no!" I didn't believe Michael was drafted. His father wanted him to enlist. He didn't ask me to marry him. He didn't tell me he was leaving. He didn't love me.

I started going to the country taverns and local dives on weekends with my sister and our friends in Wisconsin. We danced and drank at our favorite hangout, a renovated barn called The Hoot. St. Paul was hardly a big metropolis but the country boys called us "city girls." My friends are still married to the men they met those hot summer nights. One weekend in a burst of energy I cleaned my parents' house like my mom used to on speed. I filled bags with old clothes for the Salvation Army. That weekend I traded my favorite drink the Screwdriver for lower calorie Bloody Marys and a beer chaser. After my fifth one I was really drunk. When the bar closed at 1:00 a.m. we found a motel to share for the night to sleep it off.

I went into the bathroom to put on my nightgown. I robotically took the bottle of fifty-five Thorazine tablets I had saved out of the zippered compartment of my suitcase. (Alcohol triples the effect of psychotropic drugs.) I knew exactly how many there were. I swallowed them all, choking and gagging, scribbled a farewell note: "Tell Michael I love him" and put it under my purse. Still wearing thick makeup, false eyelashes and my low-cut red dress, I got into bed and prepared my dying face. I started to feel drowsy and saw my sister getting ready for bed and realized she would wake up to find my body. I blurted, "I took the bottle of pills."

Donna went to wake our friends in the neighboring motel room. They propped me up, dragged me to the car and took me to the Rice Lake Clinic. I blacked out on the gurney. Angels escorted me into the Light. I felt so much love. There were no devils poking me with pitchforks. There was no fire or darkness, only the pure Light of Divine Love. As I explained in the beginning, the angels told me to "get back down there." I did not want to leave the joy and love I felt. I was pushed back from the peace of Heaven to return to my earthly life. Other authors have written about being embraced or saved by the Light. I was goosed by the Light. These supreme, all loving angels escorted me back to my body, promised to protect me and asked that I tell the truth. I didn't know what truth I had to tell or who or what they would protect me from, but I was very close to finding out.

The next thing I knew I was standing at the kitchen sink. My father was pouring a glass of milk from the refrigerator, and I said to him, ". . . Now you are ready for prenatal care." I suddenly was conscious and wondered why I had said something so bizarre to my father. I asked, "What day is it?" and ran into the living room to look at his desk calendar. I could not remember the last six weeks. It was a dead zone. I was confused, exhausted and back to abnormal.

The only thing I remembered after being in the emergency room was looking out the hospital window and seeing Michael waving to me from the lawn below. But Michael was in Army boot camp. My sister said the doctors told her I might not survive and if I did I might have permanent brain damage. When my dad brought me home, I'm told I was acting like a three year old. I was going through withdrawal from the overdose. If it had gone on much longer I'd have been put in an institution. The angels were keeping their promise.

When the summer of 1968 arrived, my sister convinced me to attend a company picnic sponsored by 3M, where she and my dad worked. It was at the Como Lake Pavilion. I reluctantly tagged along. That evening I was introduced to Robert Petraszewski, the brother of Donna's date. Robert was a very tall, attractive twenty-six year old with wavy brown hair who resembled the actor James Garner. I was thinner than I'd ever been. My hair was still short but hair extensions were popular and I had one called a "fall" attached so it looked like I had very long hair trailing down my back. There was a live band playing on stage, and we danced until midnight. His large hands dwarfed mine. I felt petite in his embrace. Robert gave me a ride home in his white convertible. We started dating. He was on a softball team, and I often sat on a stadium blanket on the grass watching the game with his dad. It was a carefree summer. Every Friday he took me to Hafner's Supper Club for dinner where we ate food I had never had before: shrimp, steak and lobster. It beat hamburger-and-tuna hotdish.

Robert worked as a foreman at the Whirlpool Appliance Factory. After one of his games, he introduced me to a mixed drink called a Harvey Wallbanger. I guzzled it like soda pop and got drunk and horny. That autumn I had no thought for the past or future. It was the "make love, not war" era and the sexual revolution. Robert and I "made love" in his car, on the beach, on the golf course and eventually his favorite spot under a large oak tree in the park in back of Duluth playground. Contrary to the old warning, "He'll leave when he gets what he wants," we were addicted to orgasms. It had to be love.

I went back to school and invited Robert to the homecoming dance. I wore a black, short, low-cut spaghetti-strap dress with black high heels studded with rhinestones that matched my earrings and necklace. When I looked in the mirror I saw a woman, but the little girl I'd tried to leave behind was only hiding. After the dance we went bar hopping and ended up at a nightclub in Minneapolis called the Gay Nineties. I was still underage, but Robert whispered something to the hostess and we were seated at a table down in front of the stage with drinks flowing. I was feeling no pain when a buxom blonde transvestite comedian named Lee strutted on stage. I about choked on my swizzle stick. It was Lee from the psych ward. He made me laugh so hard my eyes watered and mascara ran down my cheeks. A lineup of performers wearing sequined gowns and feather boas filled the stage. There were drag queens impersonating Judy Garland and Marilyn Monroe. For the grand finale the star of the show, a Cuban, green-eyed bombshell named Shalimar, was introduced. She looked like a woman but her slim hips, Adam's apple and hard, grapefruit-shaped breasts gave it away. Robert whispered, "She just had sex change surgery." I realized then Shalimar was also in the ward with us, the mysterious woman policemen had visited. Robert took me backstage and introduced me to his friends. Lee and Shalimar didn't recognize me without my hospital gown. I giggled, happy to see them free and back in the world. If Mother could see me now.

I was writing a lot of poetry then and sent a poem to Robert. I didn't hear from him for a few days and thought for sure I'd scared him away. The next Saturday Dad called me to come downstairs. He had a long white box that was just delivered. "It's for you." Inside were long-stemmed red roses with a note that said, "Let these speak for me until I can find the right words. Love, Robert." He always knew what I wanted to hear.

In September I missed my period. In October I missed my period. In November I went to Planned Parenthood for a pregnancy test, and it was positive. I wasn't scared. That night I told Robert and teased him about being a daddy. He was very quiet. In fact, he drove silently for several miles, going to an unfamiliar area where we had never been before, somewhere near a deserted park reserve. We made love, but he was rough and acted very cold, not his usual talkative self. I remember him wearing dark sunglasses and I could not read the expression in his eyes. When he dropped me off at home he said, "I need time to think." It took me a couple of weeks to realize he had dumped me.

I tried to keep the pregnancy a secret, but I was gaining weight. My mom told me that from behind I looked like "two kids fighting under a blanket." I wanted to scream at her, "That's because I'm pregnant!" but lost my nerve. I had contacted St. Joseph's Home for Unwed Mothers and planned to give the baby up. I didn't want my child to grow up without a father and have a "crazy" mother. That plan was interrupted when my dad received a letter from Robert telling him that I was pregnant and accusing my former boyfriend Michael of being the father. Dad was angry that I had been so careless. I told him that I was taking care of it. That same week Robert called and tried to talk to me. My father answered the phone and told him to "stay the hell away." We agreed not to tell my mother until I was further along and showing. One early Sunday morning I was reading the paper when someone knocked on the door. I opened it to find a handsome soldier in his dress hat and uniform, staring at me with this tenderness I had forgotten. I tried to hold back the tears, but they escaped seeing Michael again. What a fool I was. We went to the pizza place where we had our first date. I told him about drinking and Robert and the baby. Michael took my hand and said, "Don't give it up. I'll help you raise it. We can do it together."

"I can't let you do that. I was wrong to cheat on you. After you left I just didn't care about anything."

I felt so guilty I didn't know how to accept that he really loved me. Michael left the next week for Vietnam. I wrote him almost every day. There were two popular songs out at the time, "Soldier Boy" and "Mr. Postman," that I played over and over again.

One Sunday in December I felt sick with a fever and was vomiting. By the end of the night I was bleeding profusely, moaning in pain. I had awakened my mother from one of her three-day barbiturate stupors. Dad went into her room to talk to her. I don't know how he told her but she became hysterical and came into my bedroom screaming, "How could you do this to us!"

Dad told her, "She's bleeding. I think we need to call an ambulance."

My mother told him, "No, she's having a miscarriage. Get her some aspirin. No one needs to know. It should be over by morning."

But the next day I was burning up and delirious. The bleeding had not stopped. When my temperature reached 104, Dad finally stood up to Mom. "I'm taking her to the hospital!" He reclined the backseat in the station wagon so I could lay down. I was admitted with a dangerous placenta previa; the placenta grew too low in the uterus covering the cervix. I was still in excruciating pain and cussing like an ex-Catholic, which I enjoyed doing after all the years snuffing my feelings. On Monday afternoon, the pain began to subside. I was told not to use the bathroom and lifted myself up on the bedpan. When I peed, something slipped out. I looked down and saw a tiny white fetus the size of a grub worm. How could something so small cause so much pain? It must have stopped growing months earlier, too soon to know if it was a boy or girl. I pressed the nurse's button. She came in, acting irritated that I had interrupted her routine, grabbed the receptacle and turned abruptly into the bathroom. I heard her flush the contents down the toilet. She came out and left the room without a word or a prayer. I wondered if she treated everyone like that or was it because I was an unwed mother — they were treated with disdain in the sixties. I received more sympathy when my pet turtle died. I had barely accepted that I was pregnant, and it was over. I instinctively made the sign of the cross and asked the angels to keep my baby's soul safe. Maybe someday that soul would come back to me. When I returned home my mother had several arguments with my dad, yelling, "I want her to move out."

My hormones sucked me back down into a deep post-partum depression. I hastily got a job at a haircare product factory working the graveyard shift on the assembly line. I rented a room in a boarding house downtown on Exchange Street. It was in an old brownstone building that had once been the convent where I had visited Sister Cabrini. I felt a deep sense of grief for all I had lost — the baby, my mother, Michael, my innocence and my faith. I still believed in God, but not my given religion. Living in the old convent stirred something in my soul, and I began a spiritual journey. Two of my brothers were in India studying with famous Maharishi Mahesh Yogi, the teacher who taught the Beatles to meditate. My brothers were the first teachers of Transcendental Meditation in Minnesota. They had a secret mantra and learning mine would help me survive, but things got a lot worse before I listened to the enlightened master.

Always love,

Diana

Transcendental Meditation founder, Maharishi Mahesh Yogi

Chapter 7

The Ghost of Central Manor

Dear Penny,

I haven't written for several weeks because I've been thinking about the next chapter. How do I write about the paranormal believably after my sanity was questioned? Who will believe ME? My promise was to tell the truth, not to worry about the reaction of those too fearful to hear it.

I was renting a small room in an old historical building in downtown St. Paul on the corner of Cedar and Exchange, just south of the State Capitol, called Central Manor. At the turn of the century, it had been a music conservatory and then it was a convent—the convent where I had visited Sister Cabrini with my classmates from Blessed Sacrament. My narrow little chamber, Room 7, was at the end of the hallway and oddly elevated higher than the others. Three steps led up to the level my room was on. There was a stained-glass window on the far wall facing the alley in back of the building.

As soon as I moved in, I felt the presence of a spirit. The first night I slept there when it grew dark, I saw the faint glimmer of tiny, unexplained lights flickering in the corner of the room. I convinced myself they were reflections from the streetlight or passing cars. The next day I met another boarder named Joan in the basement laundry room. She asked me if I wanted to walk a few blocks to Mickey's Diner and have breakfast. Joan was a student at St. Kate's. She knew the history of Central Manor and told me that Room 7 was built on the exact space where the altar had been in the convent chapel. Joan told me, "The spirit of a nun is haunting the place." I flinched with a cold chill that ran down my body.

"How do you know?"

"I'm a Christian Spiritualist. My Pastor, Eve, has the gift of discerning spirits. She saw the apparition of the nun kneeling on the steps outside of your room."

"Stop it, will you? You are scaring me."

"I'm sorry." Joan giggled. "Don't worry; she's a friendly ghost," she tried to reassure me. Joan was quite chatty. We ended up visiting for two hours. I told her about the strange lights in the corner of the room. A few weeks later she came to visit, carrying some kind of board game. She sat on the bed and told me she had talked to her minister about the room.

"Eve told me the lights are an imprint. That corner is exactly where the nuns lit votive candles for years offering prayers to God for the suffering."

"What is an imprint?"

"It's like a negative of a film. Strong emotions from years of lighting candles in fervent prayer are recorded in the ethers like a movie. Sometimes when people think they see a ghost it is an imprint playing over and over."

"So the nun is an imprint?" I was relieved.

"No," Joan said, opening the box. "That's why I brought the Ouija board, so we can talk to her. Reverend Eve says she is an earthbound soul watching over the convent. She lived here and died of a heart attack at Mass."

"Joan, I can't do that. I was taught that the Ouija board is a tool of the devil."

"We'll call on Jesus and ask for protection. Minister Eve doesn't use it. She's a psychic medium and naturally gets messages from Spirit." I instinctively made the sign of the cross and joined her in a prayer of protection. I told my angels to guard the space and only allow messages from the Light to enter there.

I sat on the bed and Joan sat on a chair. We placed the board, printed with alphabet letters and numbers, between us suspended on our knees. She set the indicator down, a pointed piece of plastic that was supposed to move over the letters and spell out a message. Nothing happened for fifteen minutes. Exasperated, we were about to quit when the pointer began to slide over the board. It slowly spelled the letters "S-K-I" three times. Then it spelled out a second word twice, "K-I-L-L, K-I-L-L." What did that mean? We tried again and it spelled the same thing. The third time it repeated the message, I took my hands off the board, "Stop it. I don't want to do this anymore. I have to sleep here!"

"Oh, all right," she reluctantly agreed, "but it was just getting good." We speculated what the message could have meant. "Maybe you are going to get killed in a skiing accident?" Joan said.

"No; I don't ski and I'm sure not going to start." We laughed and she put the board away. We left the Manor and went out to Rice Park to see the ice sculptures at the Winter Carnival and came back at 11:00 p.m. I made Joan stay overnight. She saw the flickering lights in the corner just like I did. "Why do I see it?" I asked. "I'm not psychic."

"Everyone is psychic," Joan said. "How else would you hear God? We've just lost touch with it. My pastor teaches people to develop intuition." I liked the idea of hearing my angels and God easier, but I'd had enough spiritualism for the night. I didn't think about it again for several weeks, until February 7th.

I was sitting at the counter at Mickey's Diner that evening having coffee when the waitress, Carla, held out the daily Star Tribune newspaper. "Did you read about the teenager who was murdered last night on Duluth Playground?"

I was stunned. She was killed on Duluth Playground, where Robert and I had so often gone. It was probably where I had gotten pregnant.

"Yeah," the waitress refilled my coffee cup, "it was awful. Her hands were taped behind her. He raped her with a tire iron, strangled her and ran over her naked body. Her name was Susan Marek."

"Do they know who did it?" I asked.

The man sitting next to me joined in the conversation. "They got no suspects yet. The guy is still loose. I wouldn't go out alone until they get him."

"I'm protected," I said.

"You carry a gun?" the man asked.

"No, I mean by my angels." I smiled, assuming they would think I was kidding.

"I hope your angels carry a gun." The waitress grinned back at me.

"So do you live around here?" the man asked. He was in his thirties, tall and thin with green eyes and blond hair. He wore a brown shirt, blue jeans and a dirty, worn parka.

"I live at Central Manor a few blocks from here."

"What's your name?"

"Diana; yours?"

"I'm John. Hey, I could give you a ride home." I looked at Carla, wondering if this guy was safe.

"Oh, Johnny," Carla read my mind, "he's harmless. He's been coming in here for a couple years. You'll have to listen to that corny country music though."

"All right," I agreed.

He helped me put my winter coat on. "You have a nice smile," he said. I didn't want to walk home alone now. The ghost didn't seem as threatening as a murderer. Maybe this guy was the perpetrator. Somebody had put several coins in the small wall-mounted jukebox in the booth and a hit by Glen Campbell came on called "Where's the Playground, Susie?" The café was suddenly silent, stunned by the irony of lyrics about a girl named Susie on a playground. I followed John out to his vehicle. It was an old, white two-seater El Camino. The front half looked like a car and the back half a small truck box. John dropped me off and asked for my number. I thanked him for the ride, told him I just broke up with someone but I'd probably run into him again at the diner.

I didn't sleep well that night, thinking about Susan Marek and the playground. The next morning at 7:00 a.m. I was awakened by the desk clerk pounding on my door. "Wake up! You have an urgent phone call." This was long before cell phones. There was a wall phone on each floor in the hallway.

I put my bathrobe on over my PJs and went out in the cold hall. Who could be calling me this early? "Hello."

"Diana," it was my sister, "did you hear the news?"

"You mean about the murder?"

"Yeah, the police picked up Petrazewski. Your boyfriend is a suspect."

"Oh, God, no; we used to make love on that playground. It could have been me." Suddenly I remembered the Ouija Board's message. "Remember the séance I told you about?

The Ouija board spelled out '. . . Ski . . . Ski . . . Kill . . . Kill.' We couldn't make out what it was saying, but maybe I was being warned: 'Petraszewski Kill . . .'"

Donna said there were rumors that Susan might have been pregnant. My God; what if she had confronted him just months after I had told him I was pregnant. Maybe the night he took me to that park reserve and was so quiet, he was going to kill me. I had just tried to commit suicide. Why was I saved and not Susan Marek?

"Donna, he never was violent with me. Robert turned out to be a jerk, but I don't know if he could kill someone."

"Diana, don't kid yourself! The police found her blood and hair on the tires of his car."

"You know, I wanted to see him again, but when he called Dad told him to stay the hell away. He wouldn't let me talk to him."

"Well, he's in jail now. I think you should move home."

"What about Mom?"

"She'll get over it. Just come home."

"We'll see. Thanks for letting me know. I'll talk to you later. I'm going to go out and get a newspaper." I was trembling when I hung up the phone.

A few weeks later, a letter addressed to me arrived at my parents' house. Robert wrote to me that he knew he had been an asshole but insisted he did not murder Susan Marek. He apologized and asked me to give him another chance.

Always love,

Diana

Chapter 8

Do You Take this Sausage?

Dear Penny,

Bill and I went to Sparky's restaurant in Anoka for breakfast early last Sunday morning. I ordered the giant blueberry pancake that you liked.

One early morning I'd left my keys to the front door of Central Manor in my room and couldn't get in until 8:30 a.m., so I walked over to Mickey's all-night diner for breakfast. John came over and joined me in a booth. I had slept very little that week. Waiting for the front doors of Central Manor to open, I listened to John's life story. As a teenager he forged payroll checks. He claimed he had an earlier petty theft charge but without having money for an attorney he received a double sentence. John had been locked up for more than fifteen years. He was thirty-four years old. I was nineteen.

The next day I overslept. My windup alarm clock didn't go off. I had to get to work by 10:30 p.m. It was cold out—twenty degrees above zero. I ran through the dark downtown streets to the factory, sucking in the chilled air, and began to wheeze. It was my last week of training before I was hired permanently. I was late for work and hurried to the assembly line. My job was to pull a cardboard sleeve with a coupon over the hairspray cans as they moved down the conveyor belt. I was coughing and could not keep up with the cans converging at my station. The foreman shut off the line and asked me what was wrong. I prayed he couldn't hear my lungs whistling. When I pulled my inhaler out of my pocket he told me to go to the nurse's office. The nurse took my vitals and told me to lie down on the cot. My blood pressure was high.

Twenty minutes later she returned with the manager of Human Resources, who handed me termination papers. I was told it was because I couldn't keep up. How was I going to pay for my room? I didn't want to go home. When I got back to Central Manor I couldn't stop ruminating. Why was my life spared when I had just tried to kill myself? Why did Robert kill Susan and not me? Why did I live and my baby die?

Ever since the miscarriage I had felt a deep despair I could not climb out of. I had fitful bouts of sleep. I had used my ephedrine inhaler too much and was shaking. Late that night I had a meltdown. I began to throw things, breaking everything I could get my hands on. The people in the neighboring rooms pounded on the wall. "Shut up." "Keep it down or I'll call the manager!"

I put on my coat and hurried down the hall and out of the building. I ran to the Robert Street Bridge, thinking the name of the bridge was a sign. I dropped my purse on the sidewalk and climbed up on the railing and peered into the murky, churning water of the Mississippi that beckoned. I was going to drop into the river when I felt hands pulling me backwards. A policeman had me by the shoulders. I struggled to get free when his partner came to his aid. They wrestled me to the ground, handcuffed me and moved me into the backseat of the patrol car.

I was taken to Ramsey County Hospital for observation. The handcuffs were removed and I was placed in a padded cell. The policeman left and a nurse came toward me with a syringe filled with orange liquid. It was Thorazine, the drug I was allergic to and had overdosed on. "No, please, don't," I pleaded. "I'll do what you want. Please, no drugs." She left the room and came back with two male orderlies who held me down on a mattress on the floor while she gave me the injection.

The next morning, I was a zombie, back to doing the Thorazine shuffle on the way to the art therapy room. I was instructed to paint pictures until it was my turn to see the psychiatrist. I knew they could only keep me for seventy-two hours. I would try to cooperate and not say anything crazy or religious. I dared not talk about angels, the murder or the ghost of Central Manor or I'd be labeled delusional.

The physician was very kind. She had a thick foreign accent and asked to see the paintings I had done that morning.

Trying to make nice, I asked her where she was from.

"I am from Latvia," she answered. "Diana, I called your father and was able to get your medical records. You should never have been given Thorazine. We have many other medications that help with depression."

"No, thank you." I looked down at the ugly, thin hospital gown.

The doctor held out one of my paintings. "I like this one. In fact, I have something to share with you."

I still would not look at her.

"When I was reading your chart I was thinking of telling you an old Latvian proverb that 'life cannot be violins and rose trees,' so I was surprised when you showed me the painting you just did of trees filled with roses."

She got a smile out of me with that one. Maybe she thought I was psychic. I wished I was. In my mind the best thing you could be was a psychic who gave people hope or a comedian like Steve Allen who made people laugh and forget their pain. But I was neither.

"I don't know what it means," she said, "but I want you to know that I don't think you are crazy. We legally have to release you tomorrow, but you can come and see me at my office any time." She handed me her business card. "Will you do that for me?"

"Maybe," I answered, lying. There was no way in hell I would risk being sent back to live in a nursing home. She made me promise in writing not to harm myself. After I finished she told me I had a visitor. I was scared it was my parents. I was escorted to the visitor's room, where John from Mickey's Diner was waiting for me. He had gone to Central Manor to see me and was told I had trashed the room and left. There was a small blurb in the paper about a girl attempting to jump off the Robert Street Bridge. He called the hospital and found me.

Three weeks later, John and I went to a Justice of the Peace in an office above The Savoy Pizza Parlor to get married. A cleaning lady and waiter from the restaurant were our witnesses. As the aroma of garlic rose up from the kitchen below, I thought of the judge mistakenly saying, "Do you take this sausage to be your lawful wedded husband?" There was no celebration, no reception. We went back to John's two-room rental on Nina Street near the Cathedral. My father gave us enough money for food and rent for a few months until John got a job as a maintenance mechanic at Fisher Nut Company. We moved into an old brownstone sixplex on Grand Avenue.

The news reported that Robert was convicted of the heinous murder of Susan Marek and sent to prison. By spring I was already pregnant. Because of the earlier miscarriage, I didn't really believe I was going to carry the baby full term. I was in denial that I was having a baby with John, who I really didn't know well. It was better to have him as a father to my child than a murderer. Had I not miscarried Robert's child, I'd have been tied to him forever.

That year my brothers, Peter and Terry, had returned from India after becoming teachers of Transcendental Meditation. My brothers told me about reincarnation and warned me that if I committed suicide I would just have to come back and start all over again, maybe even in worse circumstances. That cured me of the urge to escape for a while. I didn't want to believe in reincarnation, once was enough, but sometimes I found myself feeling familiar with people I had never met and places where I had never been before. I liked the idea of a soul family somewhere out there that would mysteriously show up in my life. I read books about reincarnation and learned that often souls of miscarried and aborted babies were born again to their mother in better circumstances. Young children often remember and report on earlier lives until they are indoctrinated to forget. I wondered if the child I was carrying now had been the baby I lost. That soul took one look at Killer Robert and said, "I'm out of here. I'll wait for the next fertile egg." I liked that God would give us another chance if we wanted it. Although reincarnation was foreign to me, I learned that more people in the world believe in it than don't. The early Church removed numerous references to reincarnation from the Bible. Hundreds of gospels written by witnesses to Christ's life, including women, that did not conform to church dogma were dismissed or destroyed. Only the four gospels remained.

I know a lot of people do not believe in reincarnation including a woman who had narcolepsy, a disease that caused her to fall asleep without warning. Was it just a coincidence she was born in Sleepy Eye, Minnesota?

On January 13, 1970 I woke up with low back pain early in the morning and could not get back to sleep. I remember sewing a button on John's coat. It was a very cold winter day. At Miller Hospital I gave birth to a beautiful baby boy we named Kenneth Dean. That hospital is gone now. In its place is the Minnesota Historical Society. I loved being a mom. That first summer I proudly took my little Kenny for rides in his stroller. The questions about the meaning of life that once seemed so urgent were replaced by the demands of an infant. Playing games with my son, I rediscovered the innocence of childhood. The greatest gift John gave me was this time with my son when I didn't have to work. When he was a toddler we played games, sang songs, danced, colored with Crayons and finger painted.

Having a child was a spiritual awakening. I loved my baby so much that I knew the Creator could not love us less. I could never condemn my son to eternal Hell no matter what he did. And so the fear of damnation that had nearly destroyed me eased and I began to heal. Thinking of my son instead of myself, I had to grow up.

Life for a while was no struggle. John and I got along okay but he was emotionally distant. He didn't know how to communicate. I realized that he did not share any of my beliefs but pretended to agree with me to get me to marry him when I was desperate. John began to go out at night and wouldn't come home until morning. When I asked where he had been, he just said he was driving around. He was a chain smoker and it made my asthma worse. I didn't want the baby exposed to secondhand smoke. Kenny was getting bouts of wheezing and bronchitis so I asked that he at least smoke his cigarettes outside. We began to have frequent fights. One day when John was taking a nap on our bed with Kenny he fell asleep with a lit cigarette in his hand. The hot ashes burned a hole through his jeans, seared his skin and woke him up. If the lit cigarette had fallen on the polyester bedspread the bed would have gone up in flames. At age three Kenny started to get asthma. When he had his first nebulizer treatment I begged John to quit smoking but he was addicted and couldn't stop. The other embarrassing habit John had was sometimes going a week without showering. If I suggested he take a shower before we go out, he'd go even longer without one. John was very jealous and possessive. He even accused me of having an affair with his mentally-handicapped brother who was slow from oxygen deprivation at birth.

I still wrote long letters to Steve Allen and he wrote back, sending me autographed copies of his latest books. He sent me his two children's books, *Bebop Fables* and *Princess Snip Snip and the Puppykittens.* I read them over and over to Kenny.

In 1972, we were living in a duplex in a part of St. Paul nicknamed "Frog Town." It had a big dining room so I made Thanksgiving dinner for my family. Mom was not feeling well. She was only 4'11". Her body was bloated from taking steroids. Her tongue sat outside of her mouth and she couldn't speak clearly. Dad said she had a doctor's appointment scheduled the Monday after the Thanksgiving weekend. Every time she ate a bite of food she coughed and choked. "Mom, are you okay? Maybe you should go to the emergency room and get an antibiotic."

"No, no it's just a cold," she said, which was odd because she usually told us she had cancer or some mysterious disease she'd read about. As I walked with her into the bedroom, convincing her to take a nap while I did the dishes, she said, "You kids don't need me anymore." I thought it was an odd thing to say since Mom had pretty much been a recluse for fifteen years, ever since she lost her smile. She'd had perfect white teeth but told us they had been damaged by the radiation and caused her a lot of pain. Against her dentist's advice, she had all her teeth pulled. Her dentures never fit correctly, making her hide even more. The Sunday after Thanksgiving we went to visit Dad and check on Mom.

She came downstairs in her robe. Her voice was raspy and her cough was worse. On the bookcase next to the fireplace was a very old photo taken in the nineteen-forties of a group of nuns Mom knew from nursing school. Kenny opened up the bench in front of the organ and pulled out some prayer books and hymnals. I looked inside the leather-bound book and read the signature S. M. Lucy. I pointed at the photo and asked Mom, "Which nun was Sister Lucy?"

"Me," she said.

"What do you mean?" I asked, thinking she was humoring me but she admitted she had been a nun for seven years in a nursing order called the Servants of Mary in Ladysmith, Wisconsin before she got married. The S.M. stood for Sister Mary which was placed in front of every nun's chosen name in honor of the Blessed Virgin Mary. She had been Sister Mary Lucy. Then she clammed up and refused to say any more. I called my brother David to see what he knew.

"Yeah, she wrote me a long letter before I left the Christian Brotherhood. She was forced to leave by a priest advisor."

I felt angry that I had never been told but I was flooded with amazing relief and compassion for my mother. Was that another reason why she had become a recluse? In those days it was a grave sin to leave the convent as it was considered a sacred calling. Why did the priest make her leave? Had she rejected him? Or not rejected him? Either way it would have ended badly for her.

I remembered seeing a movie, *The Nun's Story*, in 1959 with my sister and mother at a local theater when I was eleven years old. My sister and I loved the ending when the spirited nun left the strict convent, but my mother cried her eyes out. I finally knew why. She must have been reliving her last day at the Servants of Mary Priory.

My dad told me she left for health reasons but her friend still in the convent, Sister Louise, told me Mom cried when she was dismissed and did not want to leave. My middle name is Louise and the confirmation name my mother asked me to take was Lucy—her name as a nun. I finally understood why my mother taught me it was better for a girl to be killed than to lose your virginity. She didn't know I'd been raped and her belief nearly destroyed me. Knowing she had been indoctrinated in a very strict order of nuns helped me forgive my mother and myself. But I had to find out more.

The next day, early Monday morning around 4:00 a.m., I received a call from my brother Terry. "What's wrong?" I asked.

"It's Mom," he said, choking back tears. "She died in her sleep." An autopsy was done because she died at home and it showed she had pneumonia. The funeral was packed with my dad's coworkers. I was surprised when Michael showed up at the memorial. He looked wonderful. We talked for a few minutes. He was married, had a little boy and another on the way and was working as a mailman in East St. Paul. He gave me a quick hug and was gone.

I wanted to understand more about my mother's life in the convent. Mysteriously when she was dismissed she did not enter into public life but was sent to work as a nurse in a TB sanitarium for a year. Was there another reason for that? Had she been pregnant? Had she had an abortion? I learned that in those days, in order to avoid scandal, nuns who became pregnant by priests were often forced to have abortions even though the church was publicly anti-abortion. I eventually visited the convent. There was still a nun there who remembered my mother. She looked at me and said, "You have her eyes." She confirmed what Sister Louise told me. Mom cried when she had to take off the wedding band they wore as brides of Christ. I would never know the whole truth, but what I did know helped me to separate from her. I was no longer her "cross to bear." No wonder she risked her life to have more children. She thought being a martyr was what God wanted.

Years later when I helped my dad move out of the house we grew up in, I found a letter Mom had written to Sister Louise describing her torment.

". . . When I left the convent about fifteen years ago, I could only feel a great wound. It was such that neither bitterness, disillusionment, anxiety nor the supposed humiliation of it could replace one question. Why must this happen to me?

I knew in my soul that I had tried to live the religious life in far more intense measure than many of my co-sisters and yet it was suffocating the very things I had been seeking. I did not try to answer

the questions then nor had I any desire to do so in the future. I was too tired, so very tired, that even death would have been easier to face than the readjustment to a new life . . ."
    Adelaide Ann Findlay-LeMay (Sister Mary Lucy)

Always love,

Diana

Chapter 9

This is the Mouse that Jack Built

Dear Penny:

I've been avoiding writing this chapter because it is hard to relive and also because I know these years caused inexcusable pain for my son that would affect him for the rest of his life. I wish you were still alive so I could talk to you in person over a latte. When we got together we could talk for three hours nonstop.

John and I tried to make things work out. He even bought me a small cubic zirconia wedding ring to replace the cheap gold band he had bought me at the state fair that turned my finger green. He purchased a cute little brick-and-stucco house in St. Paul, not far from my dad. I loved the house. I loved cooking and raising my little boy, but John continued to go out at night and refused to tell me where. He kept chain smoking and seldom took a shower. I wanted to leave but I had no job, no money and no confidence. I didn't have a driver's license. I kept a journal and wrote poetry.

After my brothers went to study with yogi Maharishi Mahesh and became TM teachers they convinced me to learn to meditate. Pete had initially met the monk at a lecture in California and wrote to tell me he had met a living Saint. The East Indian teacher who introduced TM to America was celibate, sweet, funny and humble. When reporters tried to discredit him he giggled. I received a mantra or sound to repeat when my mind wandered. The most difficult thing about meditation was keeping my mind off my worries or what I thought I should be doing instead of sitting still. Some fearful people demonized meditation even though its spiritual purpose was to bring you closer to awareness of God within, as Christ taught. There was growing scientific evidence that regular meditation, as little as fifteen to twenty minutes a day, was naturally relaxing and decreased stress, improving blood pressure and enhancing mood. It was a great tool for baby boomers who had experimented with harmful drugs. It helped beat addiction and helped dreamers adjust to the reality of a world that would rather profit from war than have peace.

Maharishi made the analogy of meditation to the fabric in India that was dyed, put in the sun to fade and dyed again and again, until it no longer faded. The peace and relaxation of meditation would stay with you for a while until the stress of life overcame it. The more you meditated, the longer the peace lasted with the eventual goal of Enlightenment when, like the spiritual saints and masters, you were always aware of God's presence and nothing could get to you. Rumor has it, years later a meditator confronted an advanced TM teacher after he had faithfully meditated for twenty years without becoming enlightened: "You pulled the wool over our eyes." He responded with one word: "Silk." There was no guarantee how far your soul might advance, but meditation could only help. It was not a religion and people of all faiths were doing it. TMs purpose, like all meditation, was not to escape from the world but to remember there is Light in the darkness. It was a way of being less at the mercy of a world which was becoming more impersonal. It took me months to stop the restlessness that came when I sat down to meditate. Eventually, I had some blissful meditations that made me look forward to my quiet time. I felt closer to God than any sermon could make me feel. Not only was meditation a gift that no one could take away from me, it was the only way I would survive the next two years.

When my two brothers went to a meditation teacher's retreat in Spain with Maharishi, something unusual happened at my father's house. I was visiting with Kenny around dusk. As I walked upstairs to the first landing I looked out of the window at the small roof above the side door and saw two large white doves, with fluffy, brown variegated feathers on their heads and that thrust out like little umbrellas over their legs. I was so struck by their beauty I asked my dad to take a picture and he did. They stayed on the roof overnight, cooing softly until late the next morning. When I got the photo developed I sent it to the Audubon Society and asked what kind of bird it was. They wrote back saying it was indigenous to the Mediterranean (where my brothers were) and could not fly distances suggesting someone in the neighborhood must have owned them. I never saw birds like that again but, like the Red Admiral butterfly that rested on my breast tumor, I believe it was a sign from Spirit that my brothers were doing something special. They are still meditating over forty years later, although they are no longer teachers.

A few weeks before I took my four-year-old son and left John, I was throwing a ball to Kenny in the front yard when a postal truck pulled to the side of the curb. The mailman got out and came up the walk. It was Michael. I gave him a quick hug and backed away. He looked healthy, tan and happy. I couldn't help but wonder if there had been no Vietnam if I would have been with him instead of with John. Still an avid duck hunter, he talked about his new dog. We stared into each other's eyes a bit longer than was comfortable and shifted to avoid re-igniting the flame. Then he was gone, back to his route. It wasn't the last time I would see Michael. The poems I wrote that week were about him: *Old Love* and *Where Does the Heart Tailor Live*. And there were the cynical poems I wrote about John: *This is the Mouse that Jack Built* and *Ode to the Gynecologist*—grateful I had prevented another pregnancy with him.

Mysterious doves from the middle east

I had been writing every day and even had some poetry published in the local Sun newspaper and an essay, "Can War Bring Peace," published with my photo in the St. Paul Pioneer Press, but any attempts at being a full-time writer were put off forever. I was in survival mode. I got a job at the Central Medical Building at the Minnesota Board of Nursing located in the Midway area of St. Paul as a clerk typist for $3.24 an hour. We moved into a one-bedroom high-rise apartment across the parking lot from the office. It was on a hill above I-94 where the sound of the traffic rushing below never stopped. I had a little bit of old furniture. I gave Kenny the small bedroom and I slept on a section of my dad's old sofa. It had springs sticking out that I covered with an extra comforter. At first John agreed we should separate. We went to a Divorce Mediation Association and tried to do our own divorce papers, but John soon became paranoid, accusing me of screwing around, so I went to the Legal Aid Society to get a pro bono attorney who volunteered his services.

It didn't eat red meat, saving on my meager grocery allowance. There was a grocery store Kenny and I walked to down the hill. I used a grocery cart when I had more than one bag to carry. With my asthma, I was always panting hard when I got back to the apartment. Thanks to God and Minnesota kindness, there was a subsidized daycare in the building where I left Kenny on my way to work. He screamed bloody murder when I dropped him off the first day. He was sitting in the same place I left him, his eyes red and swollen, when I picked him up at 4:30. I wondered if I had made a mistake leaving my marriage.

A month later, when John realized I was not coming back, he began to threaten to kill my family, me and our little boy. I was shocked. Although he had not been a loving husband, he had not been violent before. My attorney thought these were idle threats that he would never act on. The first thing he did was send me a box of chocolates that had no cellophane wrapper on it. In the center of the box of little paper cups of candy was a large piece of homemade fudge with white specks in it. When Kenny reached for a piece I had to take it away from him and toss it in the trash. How sick to mail us tainted chocolates. The next thing I received, without a signature, was a sympathy card expressing condolences for my death.

Kenny playing in grandpa's yard

The second month I was gone, John quit his job to avoid paying child support and to focus on stalking me. In those days when they only had phone landlines, someone could call you from a phone booth, leave the phone off the hook and it would not disconnect until someone hung up the phone. John called me in the middle of the night swearing and threatening us, then left the phone off the hook and it didn't disconnect, so I could not call out for help. I received a new unlisted number at least three times but he found ways to get it. Although the apartment had a guard down at the front desk and keycards to get into the building, it was easy to follow behind someone and come up in the elevator without being questioned. I documented his stalking and phone calls, but I was told until he harmed me, the police could do nothing, even though the divorce papers forbid him to be within a mile radius of me unless he was picking up our son for visitation. When the threats escalated, I begged the assigned social worker to stop John from seeing Kenny but was told I could not take away the father's visiting rights for verbal threats. The restraining order wasn't worth the paper it was written on. John, an ex-convict, knew they were not enforced.

When Kenny returned from visitation he told me that John said he was going to kill me. He showed my son a voodoo doll he had made of me that he stuck pins in to hurt me. The drawings Kenny brought home from pre-school no longer portrayed happy, sunny scenes of birds, kittens and trees. He drew stick images of John with guns, bullets, bloody knives and fire. The harassment escalated to my job. Every morning, as I walked across the parking lot to work, he followed me in his car, shouting obscenities and coming close to hitting me; he laughed until I escaped into the front door.

One night when my dad was preparing for a business trip to California, John called and told me he had tampered with my father's car, threatening, "He'll never make it to the airport."

My dad did safely get on the airplane the next day. My brother Terry was watching my dad's house while he was gone. Terry picked my son and me up to visit at the house for the weekend. Sunday night, John kept calling Dad's house and threatening violence, so Terry took me back to the high rise. At 2:00 a.m., the phone rang. Concerned it was my dad or brother, I answered. John said, "Your dad's house is on fire and your brother is trapped." I hung up and tried to call Terry but the phone was disconnected. I called and woke my brother Pete up asking him to please go to Dad's house. I'd take a cab with Kenny and meet him there. He thought John was bluffing and I was overreacting but Pete agreed to meet us.

I hurriedly dressed my sleepy little boy and went outside in the dark to wait for the cab. Kenny snuggled up next to me, holding his blanket, and slept as the taxi maneuvered through the empty streets. He took a long route, freaking me out when he circled around Duluth Playground, the site of Susan Marek's murder. Had John sent the cabbie? Everything was in slow motion, as if I were dreaming. As we traveled down York Avenue, I could see three firetrucks in front of the house. He must have set fire to Dad's house, thinking we were still in there. There were two police cars and a fire marshal's vehicle parked in the driveway. The fire was out but black smoke poured from the propped-open back door. I was relieved to see both of my brothers standing outside talking with the fire chief.

As I ran toward them a policeman stopped me, asking who I was. I described John's behavior and his last threat, sure they would arrest him. They said it was my word against his. I hugged my brother Terry, grateful he got out of the house alive. He was trembling and said, "I woke up to water boiling in the radiator." The fire marshal told us, "We found a leak in the water heater. If the fire had gone another twenty minutes the whole house would have blown."

The investigator took me aside and questioned me. He said there were several boxes of inflammatory materials like paint thinner and half-filled paint cans in the center of the basement. I explained that John had placed those boxes in Dad's basement when we separated. I begged him to protect me and my family. "I'm sorry, ma'am; we can't do anything without a witness. You can ask your lawyer to contact the county attorney."

Dad was due home the next morning. The basement and

living room were destroyed and the house was filled with a horrible acrid smell of smoke and wet ashes. Terry refused to the leave the house alone that night but tied bells to the windows and doors so he might hear an intruder. The police agreed to have a patrol car drive by on the hour throughout the night. Peter dropped us off at the apartment at 5:00 a.m. I had to get ready for work in a couple hours. John had gotten by with attempted murder and arson. What would he do next? A few days later, my attorney discovered that John had been in prison for arson, convicted for getting paid to set fire to businesses so the owners could collect the insurance pay out. He had even worse news: at one point in his incarceration John had been in Saint Peter's Hospital for the criminally insane.

On Monday when I returned to work, walking across the parking lot, John followed me again in his car. This time he was waving a pistol and shouted, "I'm going to kill you and get away with it, like I did the fire." I escaped in the revolving door and ran down the steps to the lower level office. I was shaken and distraught. My supervisor took me aside and I told her about my ex-husband and the fire. She called the police. They came to work and I gave them a report of what happened. After he documented my statement, my supervisor handed me some papers to sign, terminating my employment. "I'm sorry but we can't endanger our employees."

The next day I applied for emergency welfare and received $262 and $50 in food stamps for the month, contingent on my returning to school. I signed up for business school at a community college downtown. John continued to follow me. Some days I wondered why he didn't just shoot me and realized he didn't want me dead; he just wanted to keep me from going on with my life. At first I tried to reason with him when he was shouting at me, but then I realized I was only making him angrier so I just ignored him and prayed for protection.

Always love,

Diana

Chapter 10

Assault with a Deadly Muffin

Dear Penny,

Last week we celebrated our 28th wedding anniversary: October 6th. We drove to Duluth on the north shore of Lake Superior. It's October: "Breast Cancer Month." I can't escape the reminders because there are pink ribbons everywhere. Someday I hope there is a cure for all cancer, but I don't identify with cancer. It may end up the cause of my death, but it is not my identity. That is one of many reasons I chose to treat it differently. Penny, I remember your breast cancer was secondary, caused from the radiation you received years earlier, but you believed it gave you twenty more years. That last year you suffered so much with congestive heart failure and the side effects of chemotherapy. They frequently drained your lungs of fluid. Your feet and hands were numb. You kept working as much as you could and found joy in the little things. The last time I visited you, it was near Christmas. You were decorating your tree with all gold ornaments and ribbons. I brought you some gold angels to hang from the branches and a Santa Claus dressed in a gold robe and fur boots to stand on your fireplace mantel. Your face was swollen from steroids, but you had rallied again from another close call in the emergency room. You made it through Christmas and New Years that year but were too weak to attend the company Christmas party. It's October 11, 2012, and the stores are already putting Christmas decorations out. I did as you asked and started writing last January after your memorial walk. I promise I will keep writing until it is done. Penny, I hope you are whispering in the ear of a publisher, because I'm too broke to publish it myself.

While John was harassing us, the only thing holding me together was writing my frustrations in my journal, my meditation practice and Eve Olson, the spiritualist minister who had the psychic gift of channeling messages from the "other side." When we met she was probably in her late fifties. Eve was originally from England. I had met her when I was living at Central Manor. I attended Sunday services with her small congregation that met at the YMCA around the corner from the boarding house. Eve Olson was the first psychic I had ever met. She was sweet, compassionate and funny. In my first reading she told me that in the future I would get married to a wonderful man. When I was just trying to protect my son and stay alive, her vision gave me hope for a future I could not see. Most people think psychics are at best entertaining and at worst scam artists. Eve was a special person with a sacred gift that I had been guided to just when I needed her: She became my surrogate mother. I began to realize when my biological family couldn't be there, I had a spiritual family that did show up just in time. Maybe there was something to the word "karma" that my brothers had been talking about after their trip to India: The concept that past actions, from a past life or this life, attracted people and circumstances into our lives, both good and bad. It was the same lesson as the biblical warning "you reap what you sow." My brothers first talked about reincarnation during the sixties spiritual revolution, but I didn't buy it. I wanted to get out of this place. But when I learned that committing suicide wasn't the escape I wanted, that I'd just have to come back and start all over, I was less inclined to check out early.

When my dad came home from California and found his house burned, he immediately contacted the insurance company to begin the renovation. When I told him what happened, I could see he didn't believe me. I realized he still thought I was crazy and that John had not set the fire. In fact, he thought the fire might have been caused by my brother being careless with a cigarette, even though John had called and told me he set dad's house on fire and that my brother was trapped. I realized Dad might only accept the truth if John killed me. There was another reason for my father's denial. He was in love. When he was in college he had dated a woman named Marie Duffner, nicknamed "Duff," who he dumped when

Mom got out of the convent. While he was on his business trip to California, he looked her up. He was widowed, and she was divorced. They had both changed physically—she had gained weight and he was bald—but the spark was still there. Before the year was out, I was the maid of honor at my dad's wedding at Blessed Sacrament Church standing near the spot where I had crowned the statue of Mary.

John kept harassing me. One weekend when Duff was in California and I was at my dad's house I answered the phone downstairs and Dad answered the phone upstairs at the same time. He stayed on the line and listened. John was on a rampage: "F this and F that and I'm going to kill your whole F'n family . . ." As usual, I hung up without saying anything. Dad came down the stairs. His face was pale. He was sweating and short of breath. "I've got chest pain," he said, struggling to open his prescription bottle of nitroglycerine.

"Do you want me to call an ambulance?"

"No." He insisted I not call and wait for the nitro to kick in. I was scared. Dad had known heart disease and a valve replacement. He was always calm in a crisis, but hearing the threats himself, he finally knew John was dangerous.

I still wasn't divorced. Every time my attorney specified child support, John—who was paying none—protested and made up stories that my family was harassing him. That winter while Dad was in California, John kept driving past Dad's house. The next morning when we woke up, the front window was broken. We found a large stone behind the sofa. I asked my brothers to testify that John threw the stone, so I could finally get some protection. In reality my brothers, who believed in karma, would not lie to save my life. They said they couldn't say he did it because they had not actually seen him throw the stone. It was ludicrous to see John's accusations and lies of retaliation by my brothers written in legal affidavits when my brothers would never harm a fly.

John began making racial threats to my friend Tyrone, the security guard at the front desk, saying, "I'll blow your nigger head off." The building manager of our apartment complex issued a restraining order against John, but the police still could not arrest him. I lived in a dangerous neighborhood where it was not safe to walk alone, especially at night. While I lived there, I was mugged two different times when I walked from the bus stop to the high rise. The first time, three teenagers knocked me over, stole my purse and broke my glasses. I lay awake that night, not afraid of John but concerned about gang rape—that the muggers would use my keycard and come into my apartment. No one would hear screams over the freeway noise. They had the food stamps I needed for groceries to get us to the end of the month and my bus card.

The latest verbal threat John was spouting at me on my way to school was that he was going to pay someone to throw acid in my face and blind me. Now I was not only fearful of him but anyone one who came near me. Any group of teen-agers was suspect.

One night Kenny woke up from a nightmare and wouldn't go back to bed. He climbed up with me on the sofa bed in the living room. I held him, caressed his soft hair and comforted him. Just as he fell asleep I heard a muffled explosion. I looked up and just above my head was a small hole in the window surrounded by the shattered tempered glass. Someone had shot into our apartment on the eighth floor with a high-pow-ered rifle. I woke Kenny and told him to duck down on the floor. We had to get out. I put on a bathrobe and we took the elevator down to the front desk. I was grateful my friend Ty-rone was there. He called the police, who were already weary from the frequent emergency calls to the building. They came up to my place and saw the broken window and dented win-dow casing where a bullet had ricocheted off and lodged in the ceiling. I thought for sure they would do something now but they said the same old thing: "Sorry; we can't prove it was him."

That week my brother and his wife were moving out of an old duplex apartment on the East side of St. Paul and sug-gested I get out of the high rise and move there. I had finished school and was offered a clerk typist job at an insurance com-pany downtown, so I took the job and gave the apartment my notice. The last week we were living in the high rise, on a Saturday afternoon, Kenny and I walked down to the cor-ner store to get ice cream. As I stood in line, I heard some boys gigging behind me and felt something jabbing my back. I thought it was a gun. As I turned around, one of the boys grabbed the wallet out of my hand. I saw what the teen was poking at me was a rubber dildo. Furious, I chased the kid with my wallet outside the restaurant. None of the customers came to help. When I got around the building one of the workers behind the counter came out the back door wielding a heavy metal milk case. As we ran past, he hurled it at the perpetrator and accidentally hit me in the head. I ran back into the restaurant. Kenny was crying. No one helped him. What was living in constant fear doing to my four year old? The manager gave Kenny a free ice cream cone and handed me a plastic bag filled with ice to put on the lump growing on my forehead. We sat in a booth and waited for the police to arrive. Thank God I was moving out of the neighborhood.

While John was threatening to kill us, he was still allowed to take Kenny for weekend visitation. Every time I refused to let him go, the social worker called and threatened to give John sole custody. I felt so alone. John had won. I could not go on with my life. I endangered anyone who came in contact with me. The police advised me to leave the state. I had no car and no money and no place to go. If I was caught leaving the state they would no doubt charge me with kidnapping and take my son from me. After denying my anger all my life, I felt rage.

The only time I ever changed visitation time was a weekend when I requested permission from the social worker to attend a friend's wedding in Wisconsin. John was very angry that I changed the date, even though he often promised to take Kenny someplace special on his weekends and didn't show up at all, leaving his little boy sitting on the front stoop waiting. Of course, John didn't want me to have any fun while Kenny was gone. The weekend we were out of town for the wedding with my sister and her husband Ray, John followed us. The next day my brother-in-law drove to the gas station across from our motel and discovered someone had poured sugar in his gas tank. By the time Ray had his gas tank flushed, he vowed to get back at John. I never knew what Ray did to John, but my ex-husband left us alone for a few glorious months. Then an unexpected miracle occurred. Kenny came home from visitation and reported that John had a girlfriend named Debbie. It was wonderful when she was with them. John stopped telling Kenny he was going to kill me and my family. Maybe now he would stop delaying the divorce. Then something worse happened. John informed the court that he wanted custody. He told them I was schizophrenic. We were all ordered to have psychiatric evaluations. The Thorazine shuffle came back to bite me. I was terrified of taking psych tests again.

After several contempt hearings being cancelled, often for more important venues like the judge's golf tournament, I finally had a hearing set and I brought seven witnesses who had seen John stalking me. John was not supposed to be within a mile from me unless he was picking up our son for visitation. When his attorney saw all the people who were backing me, he went behind closed doors, came back out and announced he was ill and postponed the hearing again. Then my usually matter-of-fact attorney called, extremely distraught, because someone had ripped up the original leather seats in his classic red Corvette. When he told me he knew it was John, I repeated what he had said to me dozens of times: "Can you prove it?" He didn't appreciate the irony. I felt bad about his car. He was a nice guy, working for free, but my son was being torn apart. I didn't understand the limitations of the law. My brother's girlfriend knew an attorney who agreed to take my case, so I started all over with a new lawyer.

One Saturday morning, when I opened the front door, there on the steps was a carcass of a mutilated muskrat that had been sawed in half and a note that read, "You're next." I was living in a horror movie. I called a girlfriend to come over and take a picture to add to my pile of worthless evidence.

The custody battle was heating up with John using my teenage psych records against me. My attorney retrieved John's medical files from St. Peter's State Mental Hospital. It shifted in my favor when we learned John was diagnosed a sociopath and that he had been convicted of arson several times. He had been paid to set fire to failing businesses so they could collect the insurance money, making it more obvious that he had set fire to Dad's house. The fact that he called and told me my dad's house was on fire and told me he had done it again a few days later wasn't enough. I'm sure the judge thought, from the conflicting accounts in the divorce papers, we were both nuts. Thank God my brother woke up in time to escape from the burning house. John kept getting away with attempted murder. He didn't care at all how his actions were affecting his little boy.

One Sunday when we were visiting my dad and I was doing laundry, I ran out of detergent and decided to walk three blocks down to the corner store. I left Kenny with Dad and took off down the street. It would only take me fifteen minutes. As I neared the store, John drove by, rolled down his window and yelled obscenities. I knew he would come around again. Suddenly I felt this peace descend on me and a powerful strength hovered over me—the presence of angels. An invisible force moved my hand and I reached down to the grass on the boulevard and picked up a large rock. In seconds, John was back, nearing the curb. I aimed for his face and with all the force I could muster threw the stone, shouting, "Don't ever follow me again!" It smashed through the passenger window and sailed past his head. I ducked into the store, grabbed the detergent and threw my money on the counter with my heart pounding, my hands trembling and a smile of triumph on my face. What would John do next? If he called the police, he would have to admit he was near me against the restraining order. He might just shoot me as I walked back but I didn't feel afraid; something mystical had happened. There was no way I had the strength to throw that rock through the car. I "threw like a girl."

Two weeks later I was charged with criminal assault. John had gotten by with attempted murder, death threats, poisoning candy, arson, car tampering, shooting, stalking, animal mutilation, etc. and never been charged. It reminds me of a woman I read about a few years ago who owned a bakery when road construction blocked the entrance to her shop and destroyed her business. After several months of delay, she lost it, went outside and began hurling orange cranberry muffins at the construction workers. She was charged for assault with a deadly muffin. Who could blame her? That's how I felt. I was just defending myself. I was harmless. I spent the next ten months worrying about that and the custody dispute, but I really wasn't sorry because John never followed me again.

Finally, after months of interviews and tests, the licensed psychologist's report revealed that John was a psychopathic liar. Even better, I had it in writing—I was not mentally ill—the earlier diagnosis was a mistake. The counselor wrote that I was a caring, working mother doing all I could for the benefit of my child. That report helped me let go of the past and have more hope and confidence that there was a better life ahead. I was awarded full custody of our son, Kenny. Because John was unemployed, he was ordered to pay only $50 a month in child support. He paid me a few times and then stopped. That report helped my confidence. Deep inside I had thought maybe I was crazy. That report also helped my attorney finally get the assault charges against me dropped. John was still allowed visitation with Kenny which he didn't deserve. I remember asking the psychologist how many hours he would allow his children to spend with John. He adamantly said "none,"—but after all John was the donor sperm.

Always love,

Diana

Chapter 11

Which Witch is Which?

Dear Penny,

It's Halloween. I know you liked Halloween because you lived in Anoka, known as the Halloween Capitol of the World. I like Halloween because it's the anniversary of the night Bill and I first met. This year, like always, I decorated the front porch. I bought new tombstones for the little graveyard I put in the yard with a dismembered, glow-in-the-dark skeleton spread out on the ground. I hung chains from the posts and railings, stretched white cobwebs over the bushes. Swinging from the porch on hooks are a wriggling body, a bat and a red-eyed, winged ghoul. Honoring the tradition, Bill carved a puking pumpkin, pulling the gooey slime out of the mouth and down on the steps. He put bits of a chewed chocolate bar on the pumpkin vomit. I tell the kids who dare to come up the steps that the pumpkin ate too much candy.

So, Penny, Kenny and I survived all the domestic violence but there were invisible scars. We had the profound bond of wounded hearts and difficulty trusting anyone. My son had signs of post-traumatic stress disorder, having experienced so much violence at four years old. Neither of us would move forward if we didn't learn to trust again.

Kenny and Diana after surviving domestic abuse

We took the bus to Eve Olson's Christian Spiritualist Church on Sundays. Eve Olson channeled messages from the "other side." She had the biblical gifts of "healing, prophesy and discerning Spirit." Many religions teach that only ordained priests or ministers are endowed with these abilities. In the past these mysteries were hidden and reserved for the elite clergy.

Of course there are charlatans who use supernatural ability for money and power, and I would meet some of them later, but Eve Olson was a kind and compassionate teacher who expressed love. Her presence began to heal my soul and draw me back to God. Knowing a powerful, spiritual woman helped erase the sexist religious teachings that destroyed my mother and nearly killed me. I was empowered to know that we all have spiritual help from angels, ancestors, guides and spiritual masters in the higher realms. They do intervene and rescue us when we are lost but cannot interfere in our free will in day-to-day matters unless we ask. And so I learned to pray again in a new way, not with guilt and desperation but with hopeful anticipation. When I changed my beliefs, I gradually stopped attracting pain. Like a magnet, wonderful people began to show up in my life.

One weekend, my friends and I went to a restaurant to see a popular psychic, a palm reader named David. He was very handsome and women flocked to him in droves. David, like Eve, told me one day I would marry a wonderful man and publish books. He saw me driving a powder blue car. I still didn't know how to drive and could still not afford a car. Only time would tell if that prediction would come true.

Psychics are more than entertainers. David not only gave me hope but he may have saved my sister's life. He told her she was bleeding and needed to see a doctor immediately. My sister had always had heavy menses so thought nothing of it. When she went to the doctor, they found she was hemorrhaging from a faulty intrauterine contraceptive device (IUD). That very week the national news reported a recall. Women had died from that particular IUD and some were left infertile from the damage. Donna had the faulty IUD removed and went on to marry and have two beautiful daughters. Later, when I was doing healing at a Health Resource Center, I met a woman who was told by a psychic to seek immediate medical attention. She had cervical cancer and was told she would have died had she waited any longer to get treatment. Eve Olson's reading helped my brother-in-law. Few men get psychic readings, but my sister dragged her husband Ray to see Eve.

Donna was worried about Ray getting killed on his Harley motorcycle. He loved speed and took too many risks. He had hurt his back and was out of work, leaving Donna to support the family. Ray was pleasantly surprised that Eve looked like a normal grandmother, with permed, brown hair, polyester navy blue pants and a flowered blouse. Her apartment was neat and cheerful with green plants thriving from the sun pouring in the patio doors. Religious paintings hung on the walls and she had a curio cabinet filled with angels.

"Sit down, dear." She escorted them to the sofa and offered them silver-foiled Hershey's kisses from her cut-glass candy dish. The only thing unusual about Reverend Eve Olson was a visible bump above her nose, between her eyes. It was located in the spot, in paranormal circles, called the third eye, the seat of psychic power. Eve explained to Ray that she communicated with spirits on the other side. She was a trance medium and her spirit guides would communicate through her. She would not remember anything she told him. Eve taped the session on a cassette tape recorder. She said a prayer for protection and guidance and asked only for information for Ray's highest good. She shut her eyes, took a deep breath and began to talk in a different cadence, no longer cheerful but serious and authoritative.

Eve told Ray, "I see you do not believe in this vehicle who channels spirits, but she understands. She too at one time did not believe." She went on: "A young man wearing a black leather jacket and jeans is here to greet you. He is so happy that your wife coerced you to come today. He was killed in a motorcycle accident when you were both teenagers. He says it was not your fault and you must quit blaming yourself." Ray's eyes welled with tears. He had only come to ask when he would find work. Eve was right. His friend had been riding on the back of Ray's motorcycle with him, fell off onto the highway and died instantly. Ray had been so distraught he had quit high school. Eve continued, "He is here to comfort you. He wants you to know that it could not be prevented. It was his time. His contract with his body had been completed. Nothing could have changed that."

Then Eve switched subjects. "There are two more friends here to greet you. Two pets you played with when you were a boy living by the river, a large dog—a collie and a white pony." Ray gasped in surprise. He had not thought of them for years. They were his pets when he was a child and lived near the Saint Croix River. They both had been killed wandering onto the busy highway. That was even news to my sister.

When Eve finished relaying the messages from beyond, she asked Ray if he had questions. "Will I get a job soon?" he asked. Eve told him he would go back to school and start a new career. A few months later Ray started vocational school. He was a changed person after that and Donna was thrilled to know her dead parakeet, "Poopsie," would be waiting to greet her on the other side when she passed.

I was progressing in my devotion to psychics when David the Palmist referred me to a counselor named June Beck who he thought could help me release the shame and fear from the past. I took two buses to see her after work once a week. She had sliding scale and I paid cash.

Kenny and I struggled financially. I worked as a secretary and made just enough to pay for food, rent and a bus card. But I was happy to be free of John's harassment. I still couldn't drive and used my wire cart to haul our clothes down the street to the laundromat. We wore thrift store clothing before it was trendy. We lived upstairs in a rundown duplex where mice ran up the toaster cord for crumbs. The shower ran cold and had very little water pressure. To this day I am grateful every time I use the washer and dryer. I appreciate every amenity: having a dishwasher, taking a hot shower, owning a car.

When Kenny was gone for the weekend with my ex-husband John and his girlfriend Debbie, I went on a few dates. Rev. Eve warned me about a man I was dating. She said, "You won't believe me because you like him but don't leave him alone with your son." I didn't believe her. He was a sweet guy. We didn't date for more than a few months and he never was alone with my son. About six months later, I learned that he was sent to jail for molesting his twelve-year-old daughter. Eve was right. I never doubted her advice again. I get upset when I hear people demonize psychics, saying they work for the devil, when these spiritual gifts are often used to prevent harm and give hope.

I dated a professor for a couple of years. We were in love but he would only marry a Jewish girl. I dated a pharmacist that my sister had a crush on in kindergarten. I had fun with Joe, a trucker who smoked marijuana. It was the seventies and the weekends that Kenny was gone I did occasionally smoke a joint. My reaction to weed ranged from feeling nothing, to euphoria, to an aphrodisiac, to a really bad trip that made me quit. The first time I tried it was with my older brother when I was seventeen. I went for a walk outside and everything in nature was alive; the bushes and trees were breathing. I felt more alive and thought maybe our normal state of consciousness was the dream. Joe started selling drugs and using cocaine so I ended that relationship. The last time I smoked with some girlfriends, it must have been laced with something bad because I had an experience I never wanted to relive; we were bar hopping and suddenly I could not stop laughing and then could not stop crying. I hallucinated that I was walking down a hall to a bathroom over and over, thousands of times, like it would never end. I was afraid I'd end up in the psych ward again. I prayed to God to make it stop. I never wanted to be that out of control again so I quit smoking pot.

My minister, Eve, and my therapist, June, were helping me recover from the trauma of my past, and so was my writing. I filled many notebooks. I was very lonely and took long walks, but I was much happier than I had been when married to John. One day a community college catalog came in the mail. I found a creative writing class and signed up. The teacher was Emily Crofford, author of more than a dozen children's books. The last night of class, Emily took me aside. "Diana, would you like to come to my writer's support group at my home?" I was so excited. For years I transferred to three different busses to get to Emily's big green house in Highland Park. We sat at a table in the four season front porch. I never missed a group unless Kenny was sick and couldn't go to his friend Jimmy's for the evening. Most of the writers were older women, published authors. Several lit up cigarettes, filling the porch with smoke. My nose ran the whole time I was there and I had to use my asthma inhalers. Many times I took their advice too personally and went home and cried, but I never quit. I was determined to write a book and one day get it published.

Although Kenny and I struggled financially, we had good times too. Kenny was healthy, except for having scarlet fever in kindergarten. He was hospitalized once for pneumonia and again when he got his tonsils out. The nurses gave him a lot of attention. He had beautiful curly hair and striking green eyes with long black eyelashes. He tells me now that in school he was teased and accused of wearing mascara. He was a wonderful artist. We spent a lot of time together painting with acrylics on canvas. When Kenny was ten he announced he wanted to be called "Ken," not "Kenny!" Like preteens do, he tested me, breaking the rules, staying out too late and not wanting to get up in the morning for school. I was too lenient. Often exhausted and overwhelmed, rather than fight I just gave in.

On Halloween, October 31, 1981, my friend Bonnie insisted I go to a big costume party sponsored by WWTC Radio. The event took place at Castle Royale, a new restaurant built in the Wabasha caves below the bluffs, above the Mississippi River, in St. Paul.

I didn't want to go, I was trying to forget another dead-end relationship, but Bonnie was persuasive. In Coon Rapids, a Minneapolis suburb, Bill had planned to go duck hunting but his friend Ray persuaded him to go to the Halloween bash. Bill was still recovering from a nasty divorce.

I had no idea what costume to wear. Luckily I decided against wearing the astronaut outfit made with an aluminum foil suit and a plastic terrarium for my head. I went down to the Salvation Army, my usual haunt, and found a Victorian-style, high-collared lace dress and an old-fashioned, wide-brimmed hat that I embellished with feathers. I even found some vintage button up, high-heeled boots.

The restaurant, a combination bar and dance floor, extended into several underground chambers, a perfect place for a Halloween party. Rumor was that the caves were haunted by gangsters killed there during prohibition when they were raided for storing bootleg whiskey. The infamous bank robber Dillinger was known to hide out there. Bonnie dressed as a gypsy and her friend Sally wore a corset dressed like the vaudeville star, Mae West. The three of us bought drinks and listened to live music that bounced off the limestone walls. We wandered through the nightclub guessing which elaborate costume might win first prize. There were bumble bees, vampires, monsters, robots, Frankensteins, witches, doctors, nurses, men in drag wearing water balloon boobs, the Flintstones, nuns, priests and wizards. As the night wore on, it grew livelier and more crowded. Several times we were swept onto the dance floor, finished a song and moved on.

At eleven, the music stopped and the contest began. People crowded around the stage to get a closer look. Sally decided to leave early. Bonnie and I left the room to get some air and sat at the bar conversing with a cowboy and a farmer. Bonnie latched onto the cowboy. I focused on farmer Bill. He was tall with brown hair, a thick, dark reddish-brown beard and blue eyes. He wore a white T-shirt, bib overalls and a red kerchief around his neck. He told me he was ready to leave an hour earlier, had gone out to the truck to wait for his friend, Ray, but he never came out, so Bill came back in to find him "as usual flirting at the bar." It was difficult to talk over the din of the party so we decided to leave and meet up at a 24-hour Perkins not far from Castle Royale. It was nearly 2:00 a.m. by the time we finished breakfast. When we left, Bill asked me for my number. I didn't have a pen so scribbled it on a napkin with an eyebrow pencil. The next day I wondered if Bill would call or even be able to read the smudged phone number. I remember the day he called. Kenny had just come in from outside and was crying because someone had stolen his bike. I asked Bill if he could call back later while I dealt with the crisis. Bill confesses now he thought about not calling back. He had a rule not to date women with children and he didn't even know that Kenny was not about to share his mother without a fight. Bill did call back and we started dating. To complicate things, I was allergic to Bill's cat and got asthma whenever we visited his house. Then the issue of having children came up. Bill had no children of his own but wanted to have a child. After eight years in survival mode, I had gotten my tubes tied. We looked into all our options and sought counseling.

Again, Eve Olson calmed me down. She told me that Bill and I were married before in another life. We were Lakota Indians on the North Shore of Lake Superior. Our souls remembered. Oddly enough, that's the only place we went on vacation for decades. We joke about it when people comment on the Native American art we have collected. Bill and I both

have unexplainably strong feelings of sorrow about the geno-
cide of American Indians. At first Bill said he didn't know if
he believed in reincarnation but the night we met he told me,
"I know your eyes." Two years later Kenny and I moved into
Bill's house in Coon Rapids. We have made it through many
trials, including both surviving cancer. We don't have everything in common, but a deep abiding love.

Always love,

Diana

Bill and Ken 1981

Chapter 12

No Left Turns

Dear Penny,

It is December 24, 2012, a busy Christmas. I am having thirty people over for the holidays. We have a very small house so it's a squeeze. What takes the most time is decorating inside. Our house looks like a Christmas store. My mom loved Christmas. It was the only time of the year that she believed it was all right to be happy because she was celebrating the birth of Christ. I took up the family tradition. Christmas brings back the good childhood memories.

As an advertising executive, my dad brought home large decorations from window displays. I remember a giant wax candle with large plastic fruit around it and a trio of elves dressed in shamrock green singing Christmas carols. Best of all, a musical carousel of white reindeer flocked with silvery glitter reflected in mirrors as they moved up and down. I don't know what happened to them. I guess they went to the dump where abandoned Christmas items go. When my dad sold the house we grew up in, I searched the rafters in the garage where he stored Christmas decorations and nothing was left but a few glass ornaments and an old six-person toboggan that held painful memories. My brother Pete fell off and the toboggan ran over his leg. His friends mistakenly brought him home and not directly to the hospital. His face was white as the snow and his foot was twisted the wrong way with a broken bone sticking out the back of his leg. He had a very long surgery that night with five orthopedic surgeons. They saved his leg. Thank God, because his other leg was weak from polio.

Bill, Kenny and I used to cut a Christmas tree every year until I learned I had an allergy to pine. I had asthma every

Christmas when the tree was in the house and had to use my rescue inhalers to breathe. When Bill learned we could no longer have a "real" tree, he insisted we buy a nine-foot artificial tree so big the top had to be cut off to fit in the living room, leaving even less space for our guests. Every Christmas I packed up my everyday items to bring down into the basement to replace with Christmas décor to begin the transformation. It's a lot like moving. Bill does a little outside with lighted garland, red ribbons and a wreath.

I have collections all over the house. In my office, where I always have a collection of angels on display, I set out my little porcelain angels that are wearing winter coats. I have a small Christmas tree decorated in angel ornaments and a Santa with a pink brocade coat. Large white lace snowflakes and pink ornaments hang from the gossamer curtains. An angel teddy bear plays music and moves his head to the song "We Wish You a Merry Christmas."

In the living room is a collection of Santa Clauses including a woodworker with his tools, one with skis, a fireman, and several with fancy coats holding animals and gifts. All of them have a white beard and the beloved big belly. No skinny Santas please.

In the corner on an antique sideboard is Bill's lighted Christmas village, accumulated over many years. No particular designer, but an eclectic collection of houses, stores, restaurants with a park pavilion and a skating rink. It started with a bank building from Walgreens a coworker gave me. The last one I bought was a maintenance garage for Bill since he is a heavy equipment mechanic. My favorite is a bookstore with people reading inside, especially since bookstores are becoming obsolete with ebooks. That village is Bill's project. He is more patient. I don't like packing or unpacking each porcelain house in its tight-fitting Styrofoam, leaving little white flecks all over the floor.

In the kitchen, above the bay window, there is a wooden shelf Bill built to hold a dozen Christmas teapots. In the dining room both curio cabinets are filled with Christmas porcelain, cut glass and china, most of it rescued from thrift shops. A polished mahogany Symphonium plays musical disks with holes in similar to old player piano rolls. There is a window in the box with a lighted ballroom floor where dancers dressed in Victorian garb move gracefully in circles to the music. I even decorate the bedroom with a Christmas quilt and a ceramic lighted tree my sister painted over forty years ago. The bathroom is adorned with festive fairies.

So, Penny, it is almost a year since I began writing near the anniversary of your passing, January 11ᵗʰ. I can't believe you have been gone two years already. Time is going so quickly. I realize as I write this that I have experienced a lot of loss in my life. Grief is something most people don't want to talk about for very long. Writing has really helped me heal a lot of grief. Actually, writing really saved my life, especially when I was a teenager and a single parent with few friends. I have a pretty blessed life right now.

When I last wrote to you, I described how Bill and I met. Shortly after I moved in with my beloved Bill, I received a call from Michael, my first love. He was dying from leukemia caused by exposure to Agent Orange in Vietnam. The chemotherapy and bone marrow transplant failed. He asked if I would visit him at St. Mary's Hospital. I still hadn't learned to drive and could not afford a car, so I transferred busses downtown to get to the old hospital in Minneapolis.

I was hesitant to see Michael, expecting him to be sickly, bald and emaciated, but he looked exactly the way I remembered him with his tightly curled hair and his nice smile. He didn't look like he was dying. He told me he had open sores in his mouth from the effects of chemotherapy. For the next two hours we shared the details of our lives, as if no time had passed, the way we did on our first date at the pizza place.

Michael had married Pam, his sister's best friend. He had three children, two little boys and a new baby girl born when he was going through cancer treatment. The two boys were developmentally disabled from the genetic effects of Agent Orange. He and his family had not been compensated, despite a class action suit the military had been dancing around for decades. The thought of leaving his wife and children triggered his tears. Though his death was imminent, we found ourselves smiling at each other, happy to reconnect. I told him, "I am sorry for dating Robert when you were in the service. I didn't think you loved me after I was in the psych ward and when you didn't propose to me before you left."

"I thought you knew I loved you," he answered.

"I loved you. You taught me love." Now crying I pointed to the necklace I wore that day. "I still have it." It has a bright blue sapphire heart that Michael sent me from Vietnam. We held hands for a few minutes. I felt like we were teenagers again. But we were both adults with new lives. Maybe because Heaven was waiting for Michael, there was a tender peace, a calming light that filled the hospital room that day. There was no more regret. When I stood to leave, we hugged and said the proper goodbye we never had in 1967. We were not meant to be together. I would have lost him anyway, and I don't think I'd have been as strong as his wife, Pam, who raised three children alone. I struggled to raise one child.

A couple weeks later I received a call in the middle of the night around 2:00 a.m. It was Michael. He was going in and out of consciousness, from being lucid to having hallucinations. I don't know how he even dialed the telephone number. Then he fell asleep. I knew it was the last time I'd hear his sacred breath. I listened until the phone disconnected. A few days later I was at work and I began to cry uncontrollably. I was so overwhelmed with sadness that I left for the day. That night Michael's sister called and told me that Mike had passed on. On some level my soul already knew. I wanted to go to the memorial and visitation but felt it was better not to. I just sent a card with a note of condolence to his family.

Decades after Michael died I started work as a transcriptionist at a Cancer Treatment Center. A couple of months after starting, the subject of the escalating Iraq war came up in our transcription group. The woman sitting next to me agreed with me, the war would go on too long. Her first husband had been a soldier in Vietnam and died from leukemia caused by Agent Orange. Her daughter was healthy but her two sons lived in group homes. When I learned her name was Pam, chills rolled down my spine. It was Michael's wife. I couldn't help but think that Michael had wanted us to meet. I was glad to learn she had married again. Shortly after I left the clinic for work closer to home, Pam called me. Pam and Michael's oldest son had died from an overdose of prescription drugs, joining his dad in Heaven. Damages of war go on affecting lives for generations.

I was sure we had learned a lesson not to start another war. Before the scars were healed from Vietnam, we invaded Iraq. Denial diminishes the damage done to the innocent, especially parents, wives and children of soldiers. I believe what you do to others not only as an individual comes back to you but as a group or country. The news this week reported that just last year over 350 soldiers who returned home from Afghanistan committed suicide, unable to re-live the eternal nightmare. Michael, his wife and children and those hopeless soldiers' names were not engraved on a memorial wall, nor were countless silent victims whose lives were detoured by war, including mine.

During the 1960s I was kind of a "flower child," hopeful that our consciousness was rising and world peace was coming. I remember when Kenny was a baby and we lived on Grand Avenue in a brownstone apartment, a peace march was organized to come down our street. I went out on the screened-in porch to watch. Five minutes before you could see anyone coming, I felt my heart swell with the contagious feelings of thousands of hopeful people approaching. I became aware that to feel those emotions in the air, we must all be connected. Now I am sixty-five years old, and I know there won't be world peace in my lifetime. But I have had other dreams come true—common dreams—like learning to drive at thirty-five years old.

When I moved to Coon Rapids with Bill, I was afraid to drive. I had put it off so long. Everything was spread out in the suburbs, and there were very few buses to get anywhere. It limited my job prospects and my freedom.

I learned to drive at the same time my sixteen-year-old son was getting his license. Bill picked out my first used car and took me to the dealer to show me the little Mercury Zephyr. When I saw it, I smiled. Everything that had happened to me up to that point must have been meant to be. The car Bill had chosen was powder blue. It was the car the psychic David had predicted I would drive ten years earlier.

It was just the beginning of many driving disasters. I hated making left turns. It took me six years to get out of Coon Rapids. In the summer I had to park in our two-car garage next to Bill's show car, a '71 Chevelle Malibu. I was so afraid of scratching it that I veered too far to the left and tore the door jamb off the garage. At least three times I did the same thing and my son nailed it back on before Bill got home.

Experienced drivers forget to tell the novice the simpler instructions that go with driving accouterments. One hot day Bill bought me a cardboard sun visor to keep from heating the interior of the car. He forgot to tell me it went on the inside. It was a windy day the morning I drove into the parking lot at work, got out and diligently tucked the cardboard under the windshield wipers. The wind immediately lifted the sun visor, sending it careening across the parking lot. I ran after it and tucked it back in several times. The crowd gathering behind the windows of the clinic probably wondered who hired that idiot. Finally, I gave up and threw it in the backseat.

That was nothing compared to the first time I drove up to a drive-through window. That day my supervisor insisted I go to McDonald's and pick up an order of food for our lunch meeting. It was a very cold winter Minnesota day, twenty degrees below zero. I had on my quilted parka, woolen mittens and hat when I bravely pulled up to the service window. I was proud I had gotten close enough to take the bags of burgers and fries from the friendly cashier. I drove back to the office feeling a sense of accomplishment, but forgot to roll up the window.

When I left work that night I didn't notice the window was still rolled down until I accelerated onto the freeway and felt an arctic blast slam across my face. Now most people would just roll up the window and drive on, but I didn't like freeway driving with people zooming around me going ten miles over the speed limit. I froze like taxidermy and could not remove my hands from the steering wheel. They were stuck in the ten and two o'clock position. Ignoring the frostbite forming on my left ear, I was determined to make it home singing "high hopes." Just as I sang, ". . . high apple pie in the sky hopes," the wind literally pulled the tissues out of the Kleenex box in the backseat, sending them swirling around my face. Still unable to pry my hands from the wheel, tears began to fall down my cheeks, forming icicles on my eyelashes. I made it home, stumbled in the back door with fogged-over eyeglasses and my left ear as red and swollen as a hydroponic tomato. Bill and Kenny took one look and asked what happened. When I told them they laughed hysterically.

A few years later there was a job that I wanted at a newspaper, typing advertising copy. The problem was it was at night when no busses were running from Coon Rapids. Bill told me to just forget it. A friend referred me to a hypnotherapist who might cure my driving phobia. Her name was Louise. Because I was extremely suggestible, she thought she could help. I read some books about hypnosis and was interested in past-life regression, which I would explore later. I was easily hypnotized, and I liked the feeling of relaxation. After one session with Louise, I made an appointment for a job interview at the newspaper. I found a long, roundabout route to avoid the freeway. I got the job. That one hypnosis session changed my life forever. Eventually, I could make left turns, zoom down the highway at sixty-five miles per hour, drink a cup of java, turn on KOOL 108 radio and flip the bird to the tow truck driver cutting me off at the exit—all in the blink of a turn signal.

Always love,

Diana

Chapter 13

No Skin Off My Feet

Dear Penny,

It is a cold Thursday in January; the temperature is minus six degrees. Work has had a rare lull with fewer patients coming in. I took half a day off. I put up my massage table and my son and I exchanged energy healing. He is now forty-four and learning to give healing too. My husband sends healing energy to me privately when I am in need. He is my closet shaman. Healing energy, like the sun and the air, is a gift provided to everyone. I hope more people know about it in the future to make their lives easier and to help them feel closer to God the way I do when I do healing. It's one of the few things that made me realize God is aware of us individually and really does hear our prayers. I am grateful I changed my religious beliefs to more tolerant spiritual beliefs. I am so much happier now.

There are thousands of healing techniques derived from religions and ancient cultures around the world and practiced throughout human history. I was inexplicably guided to a healing teacher I had a soul connection with. I was in my early twenties when my friend Judy was ill with mononucleosis. I visited her and brought her flowers. I placed my hand on her back to comfort her and she told me, "You have healing in your hands."

"What does that mean?" I asked. She said she really didn't know, but she had always been intuitive and felt she had to tell me. As a child I loved the stories about Christ and the saints healing people and easing their suffering. Learning that healing miracles exist was one gift of Catholicism that helped balance out the religious abuse. I was grateful for that. I didn't know then that healers do healing in the modern world. Judy's words planted a seed that sprouted twenty years later.

When I was working at the newspaper typing advertising copy, my asthma worsened and I developed bronchial pneumonia. I would get some relief from antibiotics and inhalers, but it kept recurring. I gradually realized the chronic bronchial inflammation was caused from an allergic reaction to the ink fumes and paper dust in the production area where I worked. I loved my job. I couldn't afford to quit.

At that time, I frequented a bookstore in Uptown Minneapolis called *Sunsight* where I picked up a metaphysical newspaper, *The Edge,* where healing practitioners advertised their services. I found Steven Sonmore who was a practitioner of shiatsu and reflexology, using acupressure. He worked across the street from the bookstore and was affordable.

I already believed in acupuncture because it healed my brother's tendonitis. He was a classical guitarist and teacher with no medical insurance. I liked the idea of acupressure, without the needles. Chinese medicine had been practiced for thousands of years and was just beginning to take root in America. We all have life-force energy moving through our bodies. When the energy flow slows down or becomes blocked, illness and disease can develop. Western medicine's expertise is using surgery and prescription drug management to treat symptoms. It is only beginning to recognize the energy system in the body. Ideally both forms of medicine work together. Energy healing is similar to Chinese Medicine, emphasizing the life force energy that moves through us, but the hands are the only tool making it accessible to everyone.

I went to see Steven for acupressure—my first energy healing. I loved that I did not have to remove my clothing but just took off my socks and shoes and pulled up my sleeves. Shortly after the treatment started, I became very relaxed. I was amazed to feel the energy moving through my exhausted body. When he pressed on one of my toes I literally felt my nasal passages open up. It was the first time I became aware of this energy in my body, being manipulated by this man's skilled hands. Shortly, the bronchial pneumonia was completely gone. Steven Sonmore is now a licensed acupuncturist practicing in Minneapolis at Complete Oriental Medical Care, LLC.

One Saturday morning, after a treatment with Steven, I went back to Sunsight Bookstore and found a book called *Hands That Heal* by Echo Bodine. As I paged through the book, it triggered the memory of Judy's words: "You have healing in your hands." If Judy had not told me that long ago, I doubt if I would have purchased the book. I read it in one night and wished I could meet Echo and maybe even study with her. I assumed she lived in California where her publisher was, but the next week I learned Echo lived in Minneapolis, Minnesota. There was a flyer posted at the bookstore advertising her healing seminar so I signed up.

I learned that Echo was a famous psychic whose private readings were so popular she was booked out over a year and a half for appointments. She was also well-known in the local media for "ghost busting," or sending earthbound spirits to the Light. Echo not only had the spiritual gift of healing, she had most of the seven gifts of spirit noted in biblical text including "discerning spirits" and so did her mother and siblings. I had always been intrigued by people with the "gift of prophesy" and was even more excited to meet Echo.

She was a pretty blonde who wore a long peasant skirt and white blouse with turquoise embroidered flowers, sandals and long turquoise earrings. She was relaxed and very patient. What stood out most was her sense of humor. Even though she was talking about serious subjects like boundaries, suffering and death, Echo found a way to emphasize the joy of healing. She sincerely wanted us to learn to do what she did and share it with others. Although I have since learned other healing techniques, I am grateful Echo was my first teacher. Her encouragement gave me faith and confidence.

We began by choosing a partner to practice on. Then we asked God, angels, saints and spiritual masters like Christ to send healing energy through us. The very first time I put my hands on the shoulders of the woman in front of me, I felt subtle energy coming through me and out of my palms. As the weeks went on my hands warmed up and vibrated. Sometimes I could feel the person's body drawing energy from my hands as though it was thirsty for the healing. The energy came through me, but it was not my energy. I was the jumper cable connected to the battery of universal energy. The Creator makes healing energy available to everyone. I believe God provides resources like angels and healing in return for us having the courage to leave Heaven for the painful dual reality of Earth. It at once felt familiar, gentle and sacred. I joined Echo's healing circle at her home and practiced with other healing facilitators.

It was an exciting time in my life. I had a friend who had debilitating migraine headaches. The pain was so bad that she went to bed for days and weeks at a time unable to be near sound or light. I told her I could give her a healing. I said the initiation prayers and my hands immediately heated up and began to vibrate. Within twenty minutes her headache was gone. While I did the healing, her hand flopped around in a circle as though it were releasing an energy blockage from one of the energy centers (chakras). I wondered why it didn't heal her permanently, but then neither did any of the medication or treatments she had tried.

Witnessing this sacred energy relieve suffering kept me offering it. I was in awe to learn that the Creator provided this gift to everyone. Obviously, if I could do this, you didn't have to be a saint to ask for and receive healing. When I shared what I was doing with some religious friends they were very afraid and told me if it didn't come through Jesus it was from the devil. I felt very sad that they shut out something that could help them and their loved ones suffer less. First, I do call on Jesus, but healers have existed throughout history in many cultures and performed miracles through Spirit. I wouldn't give the devil credit. Evil cannot heal because it is incapable of love.

God and Jesus don't have man's ego and would never withhold healing because someone has a different name for God. Healing energy is part of nature given to sinners and saints alike. Jesus was a healer who encouraged others to do healing and told His followers, ". . . you will perform miracles greater than these." There is a wonderful movie called *Resurrection*, starring Ellen Burstyn, that shows a woman healer who is persecuted and shot by a religious fanatic. She ends up leaving her hometown, hiding and using her gift in silence.

As I practiced, the healing energy never failed to come and my friend's headaches always left within ten to twenty minutes. Doing healing made me feel closer to God again. I began to read everything I could about healing and the tradition of miracles. Best of all my HMO didn't need to know. I could receive and give healing without telling my doctor. It was exhilarating to learn that healing was happening now, not only through saints, priests, yogis and gurus, but by anyone who spiritually was moved by empathy to use it. More women were interested in healing than men, probably because of our roles as mothers and caregivers.

I have been practicing healing for twenty-seven years and the experience has helped heal the religious abuse that destroyed my mother and nearly destroyed me. It seemed the unforgiving and distant God of my childhood was a distortion. Healing energy was real, making me aware that the Divine was personal and that I was worthy. It enhanced my life.

This gift showed me that God did not want us to suffer, as I had been taught. There are many myths about healing that Echo dispels in her book. I believe the most common erroneous belief is that healing works like the placebo effect, because the recipient believes it. Not true! Ironically, skeptics often have the most dramatic results because they expect nothing. Healing energy works on babies, plants and animals that have no mental concept of what it is. When you relieve the pain of a suffering child or pet, you know it is not a mind trick. They are especially receptive to healing energy. A neighbor's five-year-old daughter was waking up with night terrors. She screamed and cried for hours and was inconsolable. Her desperate parents asked me to give her a healing. I explained to the child that angels were there to protect her and I gave her a painting of a guardian angel to hang above her bed. After only one session her nightmares were gone and she slept through the night.

Besides the wonder of learning healing and having my friend's migraines relieved, a second synchronistic event happened during that same time. My supervisor at the newspaper was promoted. The man who took his place was not as easy to get along with. When I had my first review with him he told me that I was not going to get a raise. I was shocked because I was always given a pay increase. About the same time, I read an article that suggested saying a certain prayer silently whenever you had discord with another person. The prayer was, "The Christ in Me Salutes the Christ in You." (It is similar to the universal East Indian salute "Namaste" — The Divine in me salutes the Divine in you). Whenever the supervisor came near me, I reluctantly and silently said this prayer, while flipping him the bird under my desk. I was trying to replace my negative thoughts.

A week later, he called me into his office again. I was sure he was going to fire me. To my shock he said, "I changed my mind and decided to give you a raise."

I reminded him, "You told me it was a union issue and I could not get a raise for another year." He went on to say he had a change of heart. I believe repeating that prayer made the difference. It made me wonder if our thoughts and beliefs are continually communicated on another level. (The fact that we are all connected energetically is scientifically supported by quantum physics).

Then a third "impossible" event occurred. I was the first one to arrive at Echo's house the evening of the healing circle and I noticed she had several birthday cards on her fireplace mantel. "Oh, when is your birthday?" I asked.

"September 20, 1948," she answered.

"Wow, that's my birthday," I said enthusiastically.

"Where were you born?" Echo asked.

I answered, "I was born at Midway Hospital in St. Paul." After talking, we discovered that we were born the same year, the same day, in the same hospital, an hour apart. We were both premature and put in incubators. Forty years later I was in her healing circle. Echo called me her "nurserymate" and we have exchanged birthday cards since 1987.

That made me wonder if there is something more to astrology than meets the eye. Not the sun-sign horoscopes in the newspaper, but an in-depth chart. If the moon moves the tides of the ocean, certainly the celestial planets affect us since our bodies are eighty percent water. The early popes consulted stargazers. President Reagan used astrology to schedule his primary speeches. I know a wealthy broker who uses astrology for investing in the stock market and feels he has an edge. It is said the three kings who followed the stars to Jesus were astrologers. Why not? God created the heavens. There were more parallels in my life and Echo's. We both were authors and healers. We both had a dad named Eddie. Our first spiritual teacher was Reverend Eve Olson. We both had fears of driving. We both had one son whose name started with K. We both live in a small yellow house with a white front porch. Echo has done group meditations at Unity South Church and I have done volunteer healing at Unity North Church. Otherwise, I can't compare myself to Echo. She is an internationally famous psychic, author and teacher. Then there is the question of my fraternal twin sister and I not being alike at all. Maybe my connection to Echo was not so much in the stars as in a past life.

I must preface that I do not want to believe in past lives and have no wish to return to this rather dense, warring planet. I'm the one who didn't want to finish this life, let alone come back a hundred times. Most Americans think reincarnation is a joke, but worldwide, more people and more religions believe in reincarnation than don't. Anyone who has studied comparative theology knows the Bible included reincarnation until it was edited out by the powers and politics of Rome. I hope it isn't so, but I have had several experiences that suggest I may have been here before. In any case, there must be a reason we do not remember—maybe so we can concentrate on the present.

In the early 1990s I went to a hypnotherapist named Gary. This was the life-changing session where I recalled my near-death experience. As we continued to explore, I asked

about the origin of my asthma and was unexpectedly re-
gressed back to another life. I felt my feet were on fire and I
couldn't breathe. My hands were tied to a wooden post and I
was screaming. Next to me was another woman meeting the
same fate. It was Echo. We were both healers accused of being
witches and burned in a public square. I got chills remembering at that time Echo used her former married name—Echo
Bodine BURNS. Makes me wonder, as I come forward, what's
at stake? Was it the eerie past that led me to my next adven-
ture?

While I was in Echo's healing circle, a friend named Crystal asked me to do a fire walk with her. At first I told her I
would watch but I was afraid to fire walk myself. It was not
something you did lightly. On researching the subject, I discovered people had been burned and even a few had died fire
walking. We were bussed to a beautiful nature area to pre-
pare. For hours we chanted and sang to "raise our vibration."
We literally burned the oak logs for the fire and prepared the
twelve-foot long path of red hot coals.

We had to sign a release of liability and have it witnessed
and signed by another firewalker. It read that our hosts were
not responsible if we were burned. That was eerie enough, but
the couple leading the walk told our "fire tribe" to "use our
intuition when to start the firewalk." But how would I know
if it was my intuition and not my ego telling me to "go"? We
were told that if we were not in a state of higher consciousness we could be burned.

I was the second person to walk that night, even before
Crystal. I did hurry, but that only made my feet sink deeper
into the burning coals. I even walked a second time at the end
of the night. During the entire event, and for days afterwards,
I was ecstatic. How did I walk on a twelve-foot path of red hot
coals without getting burned? I got to sleep late that night and
woke up around 2:00 a.m. My feet hurt and felt like they were
on fire. I kept checking them to see if they were burned and
they were not. I prayed for relief and fell back asleep. In the
morning the ethereal pain was gone.

Perhaps I released the painful karma of a past life. Maybe I was enjoying the positive karma of a previous spiritual life by meeting Echo and studying healing again. In my continued search to heal myself, I was about to witness more miracles, without ever leaving Minnesota. I know it all sounds a bit "new-age," but no skin off my feet!

Always love,

Diana

Chapter 14

My Third Eye Needs Bifocals

Dear Penny,

After living together in Coon Rapids for a few years, Bill and I were married October 6, 1984. We had a small morning wedding at Coon Rapids Methodist Church. Because it was the second wedding for both of us, we only invited thirty people. My brother David sat on the left side of the altar and played classical guitar as our guests filed into the sanctuary. My sister was my maid of honor and my son Kenny was Bill's best man. I wore a turquoise strapless long dress. We had a brunch reception right after the ceremony. For the first time since I had left John, I felt safe.

Wedding photo of Diana and Bill

Once I got my driver's license, I drove the forty miles roundtrip back to Emily's writing group. I finished the final rewrite of my first book and began the chore of trying to get a publisher. I sent out hundreds of query letters. It wasn't that they wouldn't publish it—they wouldn't even read it, but I kept trying.

Every September, Bill and I went to the Renaissance Festival to celebrate my birthday with my sister. It was like being back in time with the dirt- and hay-covered roads and people in period costumes selling their wares in the villages. I loved the Celtic music, crafts, jewelry and food. Bill immediately headed for the hot apple dumplings with cinnamon ice cream while I found the espresso coffee. There were several psychics to get readings from but I didn't know which one to choose.

After meeting Echo I had taken her psychic development course and tried to increase my intuition but it was hit and mostly miss—my third eye needed bifocals. My fantasy of becoming a professional psychic fizzled like a leaky balloon. But my intuition was right on when I chose to get a reading from psychic LaJeanne Runnels. She was dressed in a gold-and-orange gypsy skirt and shawl that matched her gold-and-orange tent. As I waited in line, seated on an old cedar bench, I read LaJeanne's pamphlet and discovered she lived in Coon Rapids, not far from my house. I asked LaJeanne questions. I wasn't one to sit quietly testing her to get something. I asked her if I would find a publisher.

She predicted I would give her an autographed copy of my book. I told her the popular television star Steve Allen was my mentor but we had lost touch. I had written him a letter the year before and he never answered. LaJeanne insisted that I write him again and this time ask him to write the foreword for my book, which I thought was too aggressive. She added, ". . . something was lost at the office. Try him again and something wonderful will happen." When LaJeanne started the reading she went into an altered state and one of her eyes half closed. I later visited LaJeanne at her apartment for a yearly reading and got to know her better. She told me how the voice of an angel saved her life.

When she was a young single parent raising two children, LaJeanne found herself being stalked by a man who followed her home from a local restaurant. One night when she came home her spirit guides nudged her to park at the end of the parking lot instead of up by the front door where she usually parked. LaJeanne always followed her inner guidance, even though it sometimes made no sense. After all, that gift helped her survive and support her children. The next day, early Sunday morning, she shouted into the kids' bedroom, "I'll be right back. I'm going out to the corner store to get orange juice."

LaJeanne started her car, shifted into reverse, checked in her rearview mirror and backed up. The car rolled a foot, stalled and then the engine went dead. She shifted into park and turned the key in the ignition again. The engine turned over and started on the second try. Again, she shifted into reverse, put her foot gently on the gas and started to back out. The car went back another two feet and stalled. She sighed, put it back in park and looked around to see if anyone was near to help. It was quiet. People were sleeping in late for the weekend. For the third time, LaJeanne turned the key in the ignition, shifted, put her foot on the gas and tried to back up. This time the car only moved an inch and died. Suddenly she heard a commanding voice yell, "Get out now!" She pushed the car door open, stepped away, slammed the door behind her and smelled gas. A strange light filled the car. As she turned to run toward the building she heard crackling. Seconds later, dark smoke seeped ominously from under the car and fire shot to the ceiling, ravaging the backseat. Her children ran out of the building and reached LaJeanne. Her vehicle was now fully engulfed in flames. Several neighbors and people from the apartment joined them on the sidewalk. One said he had called 911. Just as the police arrived, the car exploded, sending bits of sharp metal and ash careening through the air in the billowing smoke.

I don't know if they ever caught the perpetrator, but having survived violence myself I felt a bond with LaJeanne after that. We both knew that angels were not just imaginary beings but rescuers who were always on watch. They communicate with everyone, sending thoughts of warning and comfort, though often our minds are too busy to hear them. If they really want us to get it, they will keep sending the same message again and again. We also were both cancer survivors. She had cancer twice, breast cancer and lung cancer. LaJeanne had to wait to have the lung resection because she required an emergency abdominal surgery first. A few weeks later when they went back to remove the lung cancer, it had disappeared. Even her surgeon used the word "miracle."

Well, I was glad I listened to LaJeanne. Steve Allen answered my letter. She was right. The office staff had lost my return address and he had also answered my letter the year before. Even more amazing, he wrote, "I would be happy to write the foreword for your book." Around that time, I read Steve Allen's book, *Beloved Son: A Story About Jesus Cults*. He described his son Brian's life in a religious commune. I knew then that Steve Allen would be receptive to my book about religious abuse. Extreme dogma had stolen my mother from me as it had stolen his son from him.

In August, 1990, I read an announcement in the newspaper that Steve Allen was going to perform a show at Roy Wilkins Auditorium in St. Paul. Ironically, I had tried to meet him twenty-seven years earlier in 1963 when he was the Master of Ceremonies at the St. Paul Winter Carnival. He broadcast his television show from downtown. Sheila and I, who were sixteen, snuck backstage and waited for hours. When he finally came from his dressing room he was given the celebrity treatment and surrounded by police and security guards. We chased them all down the concrete steps to the waiting limousine. I stood in the frozen snowbank crying as the car moved out of sight down the ice-packed street. I vowed I would meet him someday. That day was finally about to arrive.

Bill and I were led behind the stage to the dressing room door. It was a very hot summer day and I was wearing a flowered dress. Bill wore a blazer and dress pants, and carried his leather camera case over his shoulder. There were photographers in the area and a man with clipboard who asked us our names and crossed us off on the list. He said that Steve Allen was going to be interviewed but the reporter had not arrived so we could go first. We walked into the poorly-lit corridor and entered the small concrete room flooded with lights. He was sitting alone in a chair. Thinking Bill and I were the reporters, he said, "Where do you want me?"

I said, "No, I'm Diana." He graciously stood and came over to me saying, "Let me give you a hug." I was aware for the first time that he was much taller than I thought he looked on television. Bill took a picture. We talked for at least half an hour. He told me about his new book being released that month, *Steve Allen on the Bible, Religion and Morality*, the thirty-fourth of fifty-four books he eventually wrote. Steve stared at my husband and finally told us that Bill looked very much like his son Steve Jr., that his beard and glasses were the same. I was amazed that this famous comedian was so reserved. He didn't make eye contact. I saw something else I had never noticed before, even though he played piano often on his variety show; he had beautiful young-looking hands with long slender fingers.

I had thought before we met that my teenage crush was coming to an end, but sitting in that room, deep inside I felt a stirring of familiarity with this soul, not the Hollywood icon, but the private man. We had come full circle from the heart of a lonely boy scribbling his thoughts in a park in Chicago who wrote the poem that reached twenty-six years through time to a hopeless girl in St. Paul, Minnesota.

Too soon there was a knock on the door and the news crew ready for the interview crowded into the room. Bill shook his hand. When he put his hand out to me I just moved in and gave him another hug.

Diana meets her mentor, Hollywood Icon Steve Allen 1991

Around that time Steve Allen and his glamorous wife, Jayne Meadows Allen, did a public service announcement urging people to get regular medical checkups to detect cancer in its early stages. It was the first time I learned that he had survived colon cancer and Jayne, a redhead with a very sensitive pale complexion, had survived skin cancer. This was years before Bill was diagnosed with prostate cancer and I was informed I had breast cancer. I wondered, since they lived in progressive California, if either of them had ever tried any complementary medicine.

After practicing healing for several years on friends and family, I applied at a Health Crisis Resource Center in uptown Minneapolis called Pathways to volunteer doing healing with the terminally ill. When I interviewed with Executive Director Howard Bell, I mentioned the book I was writing and that Steve Allen was my mentor. Serendipity was with me again when Howard informed me that Steve Allen's son, Steve Allen, Jr., a medical doctor, had recently given a seminar at Pathways on the healing power of laughter. He was the son Steve Allen had told us resembled my Bill.

Howard accepted me as a volunteer the same day. I loved

it there. They had a beautiful garden. On the first floor was a lounge with a fireplace and library shelves filled with books on alternative medicine, health and metaphysics. On the second floor were spacious light-filled rooms equipped with adjustable therapeutic massage tables. CD players supplied with soothing music and fresh linens were provided. Everyone who worked there volunteered. I saw many participants who were dying or in pain and I learned to surrender to the outcome of the healing. It was out of my control. I was moved by how grateful everyone was. They often returned to me, saying it had helped relieve their pain, helped them sleep or gave them hope. Sometimes when someone was going through the hell of chemotherapy, radiation or adjusting to medications or a new diagnosis of AIDS, one day or one hour of relief did make a difference. The majority of the beautiful souls who came to Pathways were not asking for a miracle.

Some people I worked on told me I should do healing for a living. I wished I could. I was not comfortable with running my own business. Of course, working at a full-time job, I didn't have much time to do healing work. I guess I still had "poverty thinking." I'd been taught money was evil and being poor was a virtue, although the Church didn't follow that example, becoming one of the richest institutions in the world—though they do donate millions of dollars to charity.

I admire professional healers who are successful. Some religious people do not believe you should ever receive money for spiritual work and others say the opposite, that it is crucial the healer receives something in return. I remembered that Echo had taught us that in a healing business you are not charging for the "energy" but for your time. All healing comes from God and works through us. You can be a flawed person and even a sick person and still be given this gift of Spirit to share in love with those who suffer.

I always thanked the people who came to me for their trust. That truly was my payment—to have someone so vulnerable share their most intimate experiences and their end-of-life struggles. Unlike some healers, I always told them to talk if they felt they needed to. They usually couldn't talk enough, pouring out their fears and anger, describing horrific invasive medical treatments, side effects of prescription drugs and the indifference of people in their lives who could not deal with their illness. I saw a great need not just for healing, but for listening that was not being met by profit-based allopathic medicine.

It was an amazing year. I was so happy to be doing healing for a reputable healthcare center like Pathways. Then I met someone who wanted to publish my book. The book I'd been obsessed with for nearly thirty years was about to be printed.

Always love,

Diana

Chapter 15

The Legend of Noodle Angels

Dear Penny,

It's Valentine's Day. Bill and I are going out for dinner. It snowed four inches last night. The roads were slippery when Bill drove into work at five this morning. We are looking forward to spring.

I was going through Steve Allen's letters and saw that I had received my first letter December 28, 1964, and the last letter December 28, the same day, in 1999, but one of the best letters came in 1992. Just before Christmas I was very sick, vomiting and so dizzy I fell down when I tried to walk. I had severe labyrinthitis, a middle ear infection. That year I was making little noodle angels for friends and family and, discouraged I had not found a publisher, I wrote a cynical piece called *The Legend of Noodle Angels* to include with the pasta angels.

The Legend of Noodle Angels

In the year 1992 A.D., after the Decades of Denial trying to publish her autobiography, Diana realized that nobody cared about suicidal teenagers or religious abuse, least of all publishers. But, alas, in the stagnating silence of the suburbs, in a cosmic moment of clarity, she discovered her true life destiny—making noodle angels.

She sold her ratty Writer's Market and stockpiled macaroni and Elmer's Glue. Diana retired to her pink office and—sitting in as much of a lotus position as her thighs would allow under her autographed photos of Steve Allen—she began gluing macaroni shell heads, bowtie noodle wings and elbow macaroni arms onto rigatoni bodies.

Diana's proudest accomplishment occurred the year she realized that her noodle angels had no halos. True, others had made noodle angels, but no-one had made a noodle halo. In an effort to maintain noodle integrity, Diana invented the spaghetti halo.

Although she was never again seen in public, legend has it she was sighted twice in the wee hours of the morning, both times in early November, rummaging through boxes of Creamettes in aisle four of Cub Foods.

With the medication I was taking, I was in a brain fog and I sent Steve Allen a noodle angel and the legend to his office. The next day I was thinking how stupid! What had I done? Steve Allen immediately wrote me a long letter back saying, ". . . It's a pleasure to hear from you . . . May I trouble you to make four additional angels for Jayne to decorate our Christmas tree." He enclosed $10 to buy noodles. He also kindly added he too had sometimes been ". . . unable to interest others in the material [he] had written." Amazingly he said he copied and shared the "Legend" with friends. Twenty-nine years after he saved my life with laughter, I had made the famous comedian laugh!

I had to hurry and make more angels to get to Steve and Jayne before Christmas. The bad news was that Bill, tired of the crunch of stepping on stray noodles, had thrown out my extra supply. I was able to buy all the different types of macaroni I needed but there were no bowtie noodles for the wings. We searched half a dozen stores in a snowstorm for those bowtie-shaped noodles and finally found one box of an Italian brand left on a discount grocery store shelf.

I crafted half a dozen noodle angels to hang from Steve and Jayne's Christmas tree. I painted faces on them and made two in the likeness of my Hollywood idols. Steve Allen's wore tiny black glasses made from itty bitty circular noodles and held a book. Jayne had her trademark red hair made with curly tomato noodles. I carefully packed each one sitting in a cotton cloud in the scooped trays of an egg carton and sent them off certified, express mail just in time for Christmas.

Noodle angel of Jayne Meadows-Allen

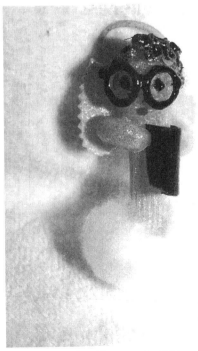

Noodle angel of Steve Allen

Instead of waiting weeks or months for a reply, I received two very personal letters from Steve Allen and Jayne Meadows Allen from their home address in Encino, California, in the Hollywood Hills thanking me for the noodle angels and signed "with Love." I would no longer have to write Steve through his office and get past his secretary to reach him. It was the first letter of many I would receive from Jayne. That began a tradition. Every year I sent a Christmas gift to Steve and Jayne, and she gift wrapped and mailed me an autographed copy of Steve's latest book. It was perfect timing because I was about to find a publisher and hoped he would still write the foreword for my book.

I had taken a psychic development course that year and met a woman named Bonita Strong. As soon as the sixteen-week course was over, Bonita started charging money for psychic readings. She was a sharp-looking, petite woman with black hair that contrasted with her exotic blue eyes. Bonita was confident, aggressive and loved attention. We were polar opposites, but I admired her tenacity. Of course I asked her if she saw my book being published, and Bonita asked to read the manuscript. She called me and emphatically stated that she would publish my book. She saw money signs predicting the sum of $100,000 coming from an older man. Bonita had published two of her own books. I finally had a publisher. I signed a generic book contract Bonita pulled off the Internet. I was so excited my story would finally reach those it might help, especially suicidal teens and survivors of domestic abuse.

Steve Allen kept his promise and wrote the foreword. Bonita printed a short blurb from this on the back of the book jacket: *"All of us suffer disappointments, setbacks, even tragedies. Perhaps, from Diana's history, we can learn something of the human capacity for survival and the ability of hope to bring us through even the darkest days."* – Steve Allen.

Despite the excitement of the foreword, Bonita was acting strange. A month before the book was to be printed, she had asked me to change all of the chapter titles that I loved and demanded I do it in three days. I was confused by her request, but I quickly thought of using the titles of songs that were popular when the action took place as chapter headings such as "Where's the Playground Susie" for the chapter about Susan Marek's murder. The song titles were sixties and seventies classics. When I told Bonita, she hesitated. I felt as though she hadn't expected me to come through. Maybe she wanted to get out of the contract. I convinced her that they would work and joked that they were perfect for the background music in a made-for-TV movie. Bonita reluctantly accepted the changes and printed the book.

In September, Bill threw me a big celebration party in the backyard. He rented chairs and a tent in case of rain, but it was a perfect sunny, cloudless day. I'd been obsessed with this book for thirty years, and my dream had finally come true. Two days before my party, Bonita said she wasn't coming and could not supply the books for my friends and family. I'd invited over three hundred people and put on the invitation B.Y.O.B.: buy your own book. Everyone I'd ever met, worked with or talked to about my book with was invited. I explained to Bonita since the contract gave her 94% profits and me the author 6% royalties (not uncommon) she would earn most of the money made at the party and even recoup her printing costs. Well, she changed her tune and delivered the books to my party but was still acting oddly aloof. Then her friend who I'd hired to cater the event backed out the night before. We ordered trays of food from a local deli.

It was a perfect day of absolute joy. Everyone showed up. Three of my surrogate moms—June the counselor, Emily my writing teacher, and Louise my hypnotherapist—came. My Uncle Dick flew in from Florida, and my Aunt Ida Mae came down from Rice Lake, Wisconsin. My then eighty-three-year-old dad, who had lost his second wife, showed up with his current girlfriend. We had two chocolate sheet cakes decorated like my book, lots of food, wine and beer. A neighbor brought over a case of champagne. We started partying at 11:00 a.m. After dark we had a bonfire in the back yard and whooped it up until 3:00 a.m. the next morning. Bonita brought me a black vase with one white rose. I could tell instead of being happy for me, she resented the attention I was getting. She didn't stay long, but she made enough money that day to pay the printer.

That fall, I went back to the Renaissance Festival and saw my psychic friend LaJeanne who was working and couldn't come to the party. I gave her an autographed copy of my book. Her prediction came true. Unlike my publisher, she was thrilled for me.

LaJeanne's premonition comes true

In December, I thought everything was going well. My book was on the shelves at Barnes and Noble stores. Earlier Bonita had scheduled me on a local talk show and a radio program. I had arranged with the assistant television producer to have Steve Allen call in when I was on the air. That day I was brought into the green room where guests waited to go on the show. I wore a white, frilly blouse under a new red wool suit with a skirt and long black boots. It was the week of Christmas and the stage was decorated with poinsettias and a big pine tree in the corner. There was a television monitor mounted in the room so you could watch the program while you waited. That year for a holiday theme, Target had a national ad campaign using *It's a Wonderful Life,* the classic black-and-white television movie. While I sat alone in the waiting area, the grown actors and actresses who played the children in the famous movie came in and sat next to me. I was in awe. They were going to be on the air before me. Before their interview, they showed scenes from the movie with the suicidal character George Bailey jumping off a bridge into a turbulent river and being saved by his guardian angel Clarence. It was the perfect segue for my story about a suicidal teen rescued by angels. I was very happy when I walked on stage and saw Bill and some of my friends in the audience and could hardly wait to tell them who I'd just met.

When the host asked me, "Is this book about suffering?" he jarred me out of my movie nostalgia. It became obvious he had not read the book and knew nothing about me. Knowing it was about surviving suffering and finding joy, I paused and changed the subject to Steve Allen, my famous mentor and the poem that reached through time. Just then the assistant producer cued the sound man to bring in Steve Allen's call from LA. To my surprise, Steve not only said publicly he supported my book, but he told the interviewer that he had written several movie producers and was trying to get me a film offer. The struggle was over. I blurted, "I love you" and without a beat Steve Allen said, "Jayne and I send our love."

As I stepped off the platform to leave, I could not wipe the smile off my face and then a young stagehand asked me to autograph a copy of my book: a perfect ending to a magical day. The only odd thing was that the producer was miffed because Bonita Strong had not shown up. I really didn't see why she needed to be there. The radio program that week went even better. My son Ken called in on the air and said he was proud of me. The interviewer this time had read my book and said she couldn't put it down. She played the music from the chapter titles during break including at the end John Lennon's "Imagine" with the fitting lyrics "imagine no religion." Locally people were asking for my book after the radio show. A week later, right out of my fantasy, I received a phone call from a movie producer who had been contacted by Steve Allen. He wanted to make my book into a true story TV movie and offered me a contract for $100,000. It was the exact amount Bonita had predicted would come to us from an older gentleman that had to be Steve Allen.

The enthusiastic movie producer insisted I hire an "entertainment attorney" to look over my book contract to see if the publisher had any rights to the movie before he sent out the contract to her or me. Her contract made no mention of film rights, but it did suggest vague "media rights." I was hesitant, knowing Bonita would be furious if I consulted a lawyer, which I should have done in the first place, but I did what the producer asked. I even contacted the Minnesota Film Board. They expressed interest in offering the filmmaker an incentive package to produce the movie on location in St. Paul where the murder took place. The haunted manor was just two doors down from the famous Fitzgerald Theater where Garrison Keillor taped his popular radio show *Prairie Home Companion*.

The next week the magic began to fade. One of Bonita's employees called to warn me that Bonita was going through an unexpected divorce and planning to move out of state. She told me Bonita was angry that she had spent the money to publish my book in the first place. Being a "triple Scorpio," Bonita had a reputation for revenge and told this employee she had no intention of promoting my book. I thought this person was exaggerating, but the next day I received a very strange letter from Bonita's financial advisor, who Bonita had bragged had a crush on her—but she had no interest in him. He accused me of causing her financial ruin and even destroying her marriage by having her publish my book. Shocked by his accusations, I didn't know what to do next. In a moment of haste, I wrote a quick note to Bonita's broker, telling him when dealing with her he needed to use his "brain and not his cock" and mailed it off. The next week Bonita informed me that the television interview would not be aired, that they had "lost" the videotape. I was devastated after getting Steve Allen to call in the show and having the *Wonderful Life* segue—something that could not be recreated.

I called Bonita and told her I was aware her house was up for sale and she was moving and I offered to buy the book rights from her if she no longer wanted to be involved in marketing my book. But Bonita had no intention of selling me the book back. Ironically, it could have been a win/win situation. The same week the movie producer had his lawyers look at my contract. They decided my book deal was too vague, and he would just call the publisher and offer her half of the movie deal. I told him that she had already stopped promoting the book after only four months. He believed with the new offer, where she could make money on the book and movie, he could get her to reconsider. I told him to go ahead. He knew the business, but he didn't know Bonita Strong.

Three months later, the movie producer called to tell me that Bonita had refused to sign the movie option demanding more money up front, even though he offered $100,000, the exact amount she predicted would come to her. Getting a movie made is a long process and no one is paid that early in the game. He was furious and told me he had dealt with many prima donnas in Hollywood but no one as vicious as Bonita Strong. He asked me to consult a litigator and fight for the rights to the book and movie. He and Steve Allen would back me up. Bill and I agreed to fight and found a law firm that specialized in entertainment law. We told them we could not spend more than $10,000. They demanded a retainer of $10,000 upfront, and we refinanced our home, taking out a second mortgage. I felt guilty having Bill pay for my dream, but he stood by me for the next year and a half. Our attorneys warned us that the hearing would be before an arbitrator, not a judge, and they typically favored business owners.

We had exhausted all efforts to settle with Bonita who had moved to the West coast and hired an LA attorney. The hearing went on for eleven hours. Three of Bonita's former employees testified against me, lying right in front of me. I was hurt because I had never done anything to harm any of these people, whom I thought were my friends. I realized Bonita must have manipulated them in the same way she had manipulated me. They all had pretended to be so spiritual, but I guess they really didn't believe in karma, that what you do returns to you, after all. If we could prove Bonita was broke when she quit promoting the book, my contract with her was automatically insolvent. Her broker had a neat slide show presentation with charts and grafts showing Bonita's phony funds. In evidence, we showed the letter from the broker quoting him as saying "you ruined Bonita financially." Unfortunately, I'd forgotten to tell my attorneys about my little note. When her attorney read ". . . use your brain and not your cock," the arbitrator frowned, but the court reporter laughed and winked at me.

When someone who read my book called me at home, I learned that Bonita even withheld the fan mail sent to me. The arbitrator did insist Bonita send me any letters she had received. When I finally got the letters, I read that a fan wanted to have lunch with me. When I called her house, I was sad to learn that she died of breast cancer before I could meet her, which is even more poignant now after I have survived breast cancer.

In the end, we were exhausted but we were sure, with the movie producer's affidavit describing Bonita's unprofessional behavior, we would at least win the movie option. A month later, we received two pieces of registered mail. One was from the court judgment declaring we had lost all book and movie rights. The other was from our attorneys, charging us fees totaling $33,000. Bill and I cried. We lost and were still expected to pay an exorbitant amount of money. We immediately faxed the law firm to "cease and desist" and close the case now, before incurring any further expenses. My sister told my dad what happened and he gave us a check for $10,000 to help pay the invoice. Months later the litigator sympathized with us and renegotiated the bill with the firm, dropping it to $15,000.

For the next two years we were able to deduct attorney fees as a business expense from taxes, helping ease the debt.

The litigator kindly sent my book to Hazelden, self-help publishers, hoping they might buy it from Bonita. They didn't respond, but that year I had two other small publishers interested in re-publishing it. One was a gifted Native American author who called me. He understood what religious abuse was. His baby sister had been taken away from his family by the state. Because of their spiritual beliefs honoring the Earth, the Lakota were discriminated against, called "savages." The little girl was taken to a Catholic boarding school where she mysteriously died. It broke my heart that he could not publish my book. He had the same intention as I had, to heal survivors. But I didn't own the rights, and Bonita could not be bought. She was even more interested in stopping me than earning money.

I felt betrayed by the legal system, similar to the way I felt when the judge allowed my abusive husband to still have visitation with my then five-year-old son. In retrospect, I admit I was partially at fault for being so trusting in the first place and should have hired an attorney when I received the publishing contract, not after the movie offer. I know Bonita was angry just because I exercised my right to hire an attorney. Years later, she offered to sell me the rights back. I had an attorney write up the agreement, but she backed out. I never knew why.

Eight years after I had lost the legal rights to the book and movie, my friend Mercedes and I went to a shaman named Timothy Cope to do a ceremony to ask the Universe to release my book and return it back to me. In the two-hour drumming ceremony, I was deeply moved by a vision. I climbed a mountain of rocks, reached the top of the summit and grabbed my book back. When I came out of the trance tears were streaming down my face. A few weeks later I received a letter from Bonita Strong simply stating in one short sentence that all legal rights to my book would revert back to me. I believe the spiritual ceremony had finally released the book to its rightful owner. I was grateful that Bonita perhaps had a change of heart finally ending some bad karma. I felt another reason it had never worked out was because my intention was to give others hope and her intention was greed. The sad truth was there would never be another movie offer.

Ironically, as I was writing this, I received a four-page letter in the mail from a woman who purchased my book at a book swap, telling me how much hope it gave her, twenty years after it was printed. You know, Penny, maybe it's not over. Bonita psychically claimed to see money attached to it. Sorry Bonita; wrong book!

Always love,

Diana

Chapter 16

Waking Marco

Dear Penny,

After I lost the book and movie rights, I quit writing for some time and turned my attention to healing. That was when I met Marco Morelli, a twenty-eight-year-old Golden Gloves boxer in a coma. Angie, a transcriptionist I worked with, was his cousin. She had a newspaper article hanging in her cubicle with a photo of Marco's mom, Eunice, holding his hand and his dad, Matt, talking to his unconscious son. The love on his parents' faces moved me. I told Angie I would give Marco free healing if his parents were open to it. I was surprised and excited that they agreed.

Golden Gloves Boxer Marco's Benefit

Marco had been in a motor vehicle accident around 2:00 a.m. December 3, 1993. His truck slid on the ice, flew across the median and rolled into the ditch. Marco's body was ejected through the broken window onto the frozen earth, slamming his head into the ground. He was unconscious and aspirating vomit into his lungs, choking to death. Skip Frietag, a trained paramedic, was driving by when Marco's car flew over the median. He immediately stopped to help. Risking liability, Skip gently moved Marco's head to the side and cleared his throat so he could breathe and waved down a passing trucker who called 911. Minutes later, a Medevac helicopter transported Marco to Ramsey Hospital.

Marco had a severe closed head injury. His brain swelled. A ventriculoscopy was done to stop the cerebral spinal leak and a lumbar drain and shunt inserted to relieve the pressure on his brain. Marco developed meningitis. After several weeks in a coma, the hospital transferred him to a nursing home. The family was told he would never wake up. One physician advised them to do themselves a favor and forget about him.

Then his mom heard about a little-known rehabilitation program, called A Chance to Grow, designed for brain injured patients. They had developed a specific stimulation therapy that helped people emerge from a coma but it required a mind-boggling commitment of time and manpower, more than eighty volunteers working in shifts moving a heavy slumbering body, exercising limbs and stimulating the senses. If there was anyone that could elicit such a commitment, it was the Morelli family. Matt and Eunice took their son home against medical advice. Their relatives had lived on the east side of St. Paul for decades and an army of friends and neighbors converged at the small house on Atlantic Street. Their friend, columnist Don Boxmeyer, printed Marco's story in the St. Paul Pioneer Press—the story I saw at Angie's desk. Soon the rehab program began with six volunteers working six-hour shifts, six days a week. The entire lower level of the house was transformed into a therapy center for Marco.

The Sunday morning I met Marco, the entire family was there to watch. During a healing my hands heat up and vibrate but there is really nothing to see. It is a very private experience. I was afraid they were expecting me to raise Marco up like Christ raised Lazarus.

The young man was lying in a black leather recliner. He had an IV drip attached to his hand, a tracheotomy wound in his neck and a feeding tube in his belly. His mouth was constantly moving in a chewing motion. A towel was placed under his chin to catch drool. Every day his mother had to melt down plastic mouth guards, forming them into sticks to gnaw on so he would not grind down all his teeth. Marco chewed through eight a day. His coach, Moose, who came every morning to help lift him into the therapy pool, got a discount for the mouth guards at a local sporting goods store.

I explained a little about energy healing and put my CD of flute music, by Nakai, on my boom box. I went back to the chair and placed my hands on Marco's soft, gleaming black hair. He was so young! After doing healing for years, my hands immediately heated up even before I prayed for the healing to come. It flowed through my palms and like a magnet Marco's body pulled the gentle energy in. One of his brothers, who was holding Marco's cold feet, said he felt them warm up as I worked.

I was overwhelmed by the love. No church could hold more angels than were present there. I was happy when Matt invited me back but the next week when I returned he said the healing made "Marco worse," and invited me upstairs to have a "talk." I was glad he was willing to talk about it. I believe Matt's son had a difficult week but it was doubtful it was connected to the healing. The beauty of healing energy is that it is not harmful. On rare occasions recipients might have what is called a "healing crisis" where they may feel tired or a bit worse before they get better, similar to when you sometimes spike a fever just before you get better.

I said a silent prayer: "God if you want me to come here, help me now." I wasn't driving fifty miles roundtrip on my day off if I wasn't welcome. I understood how Matt felt. I had not been completely healed myself.

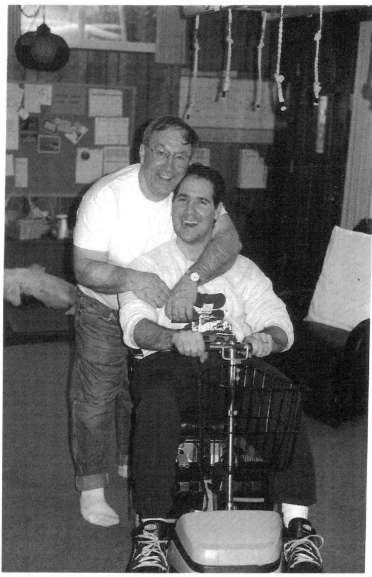

Marco Morelli and dad Matt

I told Matt, "I know you didn't get the miracle you hoped for, but I don't think the healing made Marco worse. Why don't you let me give you a healing and see how it feels and then decide if you want Marco to have more?"

"Okay," Matt agreed and flopped down in his recliner in the living room. His brother Gino and eighty-seven-year-old mom watched from the kitchen. Amused, Gino razzed Matt, saying, "Hey, you getting a massage?"

Matt, a retired plumber for the city, was exhausted from the constant stress of caring for his son and not knowing if he would improve. He had a hernia from lifting Marco but couldn't take the time to get it repaired. He wore a white T-shirt. Red suspenders held up his khaki pants. He seemed surprised when he felt the heat and energy and commented, "It's like a little motor." When part of the body had received enough energy, my hands stopped vibrating. When I moved them to another spot they started up again. Matt accepted me that day and even asked for occasional healings for himself when his feet hurt.

When the Morellis realized the limitations of Western medicine, they opened up to other complementary therapies like cranial sacral therapy, chiropractic care and acupuncture. When Marco finally opened his eyes, they wandered and jiggled and would not focus. The physicians, often pessimistic, said he would never see correctly. But Dr. Ming, who made house calls, gave Marco acupuncture. The strategically-placed needles straightened Marco's wandering eyes permanently. Then he worked on Marco's crooked grin, giving him his smile back. After several months of multiple therapies, the constant chewing completely stopped. Marco began to move his limbs on his own. The reporter wrote more stories in the paper about his progress and Marco became the poster boy for the A Chance to Grow program.

Diana and Marco Morelli

For the first two years I visited Marco every Saturday. I grew to know Matt and Eunice as well as Marco and was always amazed by their high spirits and endless patience. The doctors said Marco would never get off his feeding tube or regain his gag reflex, but again he defied the odds and began to drink and eat solid food. Eventually they closed the scarred openings in his neck and belly. With daily six-hour workouts, Marco gained upper arm strength, and with guard rails was able to transfer himself into the bathroom and the tub. The cases of liquid protein and diapers disappeared from the basement.

I learned so much from Marco. Instead of yelling at my body for being too fat, for needing glasses, for frizzy hair (depending on the humidity my hair either looks like Carole King or Don King), I began to appreciate the miracle of a functioning body. I began to be grateful for things I had taken for granted: eating, walking, talking, remembering and using the bathroom.

The third year I visited Marco, he had a serious relapse, having several bouts of bronchitis and pneumonia. His brain was falling where his skull had cracked and he needed risky neurosurgery to repair it. He was weak and everyone wondered how far surgery might set him back after all his progress. Driving home, I prayed for a sign that Marco would survive the operation.

The next Saturday the answer came when Matt opened a magazine and showed me a full-page color advertisement in a national sports magazine. In the photo was a boxer alone in an old gymnasium, punching a Heavy Bag. There were leaded windows from ceiling to floor. Sunlight streamed through, illuminating the figure in light. It was a photo of Marco working out in the 10th Street Gym, taken before the accident six years earlier. The photographer had placed it in his portfolio and moved to New York, eventually selling it for a national ad campaign for a popular deodorant. Suddenly Marco's photo was everywhere, in magazines, movie theaters and it appeared on coupons for the antiperspirant in every Sunday paper. The ad copy at the side of the photo, written by a public

relations firm that didn't know anything about Marco read:
No trendy Health Club.
No Bull.
110% Protection.
. . . JUST LIKE YOU, IT NEVER QUITS!

Our sign had come. He had the neurosurgery, came home with chemical-induced hepatitis, struggled through it, resumed his steady progress and never quit.

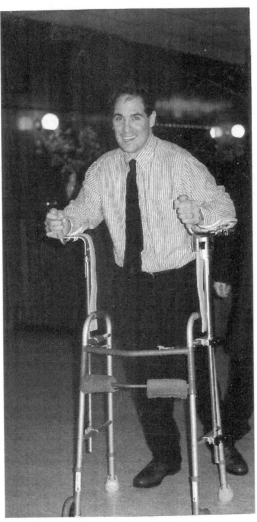

Marco walking at volunteer party

In 1998, at the Morellis Annual Volunteer Christmas Dinner, Marco walked on the dance floor with his walker. He let go of the metal stand and stood with me for a slow dance. Our faces touching, we swayed from side to side to the live music. I had to let go of Marco and give the girls lined up and waiting to dance with him their chance. We celebrated how far he had come. Because he was in a coma for so long, his balance and speech never completely returned. Maybe souls take on physical or mental challenges in life to teach us to look deeper, beyond the package of the body into the soul. Public advocates like quadriplegic Christopher Reeve; Michael J. Fox with Parkinson's or Evangelist Nick Vujicic—born with no arms or legs—inspire us to endure challenges and keep going.

When I worked with Marco, I learned to pray more. As a teenager I thought God never heard us because my prayers for my mother's health never came true. I have come to believe that the thousands of prayers that went up to heaven for Marco really did help him through the toughest days. During that time, I still belonged to Echo's healing circle where we sent "distant healing" for those who asked. In my day job, I worked with a woman who asked our group to pray for Jason, her eighteen-month-old baby. He had contracted encephalitis from an infected mosquito. He was unconscious and not expected to survive. The group of twelve focused healing on Jason around 9:20 a.m. Saturday and went on with our prayers. The next Monday at work, his mother told me her son had emerged from the coma and opened his eyes on Saturday morning. When I asked her what time, she said at 9:20 a.m., the same time our prayers were sent. Jason recovered with no lasting brain damage. Many silent miracles happen when we align our intentions with Divine Love, especially in group prayer.

After six years and over 200 visits to the home on Atlantic Street, I said goodbye to the Morellis. Through their courage, humility and forgiveness, they had helped heal my grief and taught me how to live in the present. I had a lingering fear of Catholicism, but Matt and Eunice, devout Catholics, showed me what real faith is and eased my angst. Marco's mom summed it up perfectly in her Christmas letter to the volunteers when she wrote, "...This is for sharing with those who have no trouble accepting miracles, who don't require explanations, who believe in love, generosity and the wonder of life!"

Always love,

Diana

Chapter 17

The Big Hand Era

Dear Penny,

I'm due for another mammogram and procrastinating. How would I finish a book on healing if the cancer is back? We all have to get home some way. Even those Christ healed eventually moved on. People say we have a contract with the body, and whatever we do in between just gets us to that same point. We're born with the angels and leave this life in their arms.

After my first book was published, I was asked what religion I am since I am no longer Catholic. I'd have to say as an old joke goes, "I am a Frisbeetarian—I believe when you die your soul sails up on the roof and you can't get it down." I have found Christian churches I like that aren't dogmatic and believe in healing, like Unity or the Spiritualist Church, but I have heard too many bad sermons from unenlightened priests to join one religion. I no longer believe God demands worship or loves us less if we don't believe. That fear is carried on from the dark ages when men defined God in male terms as a dictator. I think God is more a Divine Mother who does not deny anyone the sun, the air, healing or Heaven. It is humans, not God, who would lock us out and demand a gated community.

I volunteered in a hospice program in the late 1990s to go to homes of the dying and give them healing. I did learn the signs of dying and it helped me get closer to my father the last six months he was alive. In his seventies, Dad had prostate cancer but didn't tell us at first. It had spread by the time it was found so they did not remove his prostate, but instead he had an orchiectomy removing his testicles, which produce testosterone believed to feed prostate cancer. He called me after the procedure sounding drugged on medication and said, "I just want you to know why my voice is higher." He never said another word about it for ten years until he passed out at home. His hemoglobin had dropped to six, from a normal fourteen. I was grateful his girlfriend was with him. He had colon cancer. They took out the malignant section of his intestines and again he was fine. He sold his house and moved into the upper duplex owned by his girlfriend and went on with his life. He never had chemotherapy or radiation.

In 1998, when he was eighty-eight, he told me the cancer was in his bones and brain and he was beginning to have some pain. Right up to the last month he still edited the 3M retirement newsletter and drove his car. That spring I had gone to a Whole Life Expo and received a psychic reading from a Native American I had never met. He predicted someone close to me would pass over in September and I would inherit money. It had to be my father. I hoped Dad had more time, but I made an effort to be there more and tell him I loved him. I appreciated Dad's dedication to my sick mother, to his job and to his family. He was conservative and I was liberal, but I knew the conscientious way he lived his life, with responsibility and purpose, had given me the stability that I needed, especially having a chronically ill mother who had turned away from life. I teased Dad that my mother and his second wife would be there fighting over him when he passed over, not to mention all his other girlfriends. I told him to give me a sign when he got there and he smiled.

My dad loved puns. He told us when he was in college one summer he worked at the Green Giant factory where they canned vegetables. He said, "I worked there all summer and never took a pea!"

In September, my dad began to turn inward. He had been a musician but no longer wanted to hear the jazz music he had always listened to. He loved key lime pie, but when I brought him a piece he didn't want it, saying, ". . . Everything I eat tastes metallic." He had been a proud man. One day when I visited, I learned he was incontinent and had to have his girlfriend change his diapers, but he was not angry or ashamed. He just smiled the sweetest smile and emanated a peace I had never seen in him before. It was then I felt what I had learned was true; the angels were there preparing him for his transition. People often avoid visiting someone who is dying but it is a sacred gift to be present. I think we have it all mixed up. The soul being born cries leaving Heaven and the soul taking off celebrates going home.

My dad wanted to die at his own place, but his girlfriend did not want hospice there and called the ambulance to take him to the hospital. I watched my husband, son, brother and one of the paramedics lift him up in a chair, wrap him in a blanket covering his head and carry him down the steep steps outside. He looked like a smiling Buddha. The next Sunday when we visited he said he couldn't feel his feet and asked Bill to rub them. I believe the soul goes in and out of the body at the end, preparing to make its escape. Honoring his beliefs, I asked him if he wanted the hospital chaplain, a Catholic priest, to give him the last rites. He agreed. I could visibly see his body relax and become less rigid after the anointing with oil. That night when his pain increased they gave him more morphine, drugging him into a deep sleep.

Some people feel guilty when they are not present at a loved one's side when they die. Other times, people cling to the dying, but if we can't let go we hold them back, and sometimes they sneak out when we are out of the room. No matter what religion or politics you wear, the label comes off with your body and the play is over. Lots of people believe in Hell, but I think that is a misinterpretation. There is an astral level where darkness is trapped between Earth and Heaven and people who have witnessed this confuse it for Hell. A soul can get stuck for a while, especially if it is "God-fearing." Ghost-busting may be funny, but releasing souls from being trapped is sacred work. The most comforting book I've read that describes patients' pre-death visitations with angels and deceased relatives is *Into the Light*, written by hospice director John Lerma, M.D.

On a Monday morning as I pulled into the parking lot at work, an old song I loved came on the radio about the spirit in the sky going up to Heaven when you die, making me think of my dad. As soon as I entered the building, I was told I had a call from the nurse at the hospital that Dad was dying and to come immediately. My family surrounded my dad. I held his hand and whispered he could let go. A single tear fell down his cheek and he was gone.

That night when I called my best friend Marta to tell her, she asked what time he passed over. It was at 9:10 a.m. She said that was odd because she had just put a new battery in her watch the week before but it stopped that morning at exactly 9:10 a.m. Maybe it was my dad acknowledging, "Here's your sign. I made it." Her watch inexplicably started again that night. When the visitation at the funeral home ended, we invited people to his bachelor pad to celebrate his life. We had a good laugh, realizing cancer hadn't stopped Dad's fun, when I found a penile pump in his desk drawer. Dad might comment it was HARD to say goodbye. At the memorial service the chaplain from the hospital gave a very short eulogy. Meaning to say Dad was a musician in an orchestra during the big band era, he slipped and said, "big hand era." I pictured a generation of people with giant hands and tried not to laugh—like in a *Far Side* cartoon.

When the funeral flowers died, we were left with the emptiness. When a good parent is gone, we feel a deep loss that someone who loved us, in a way no one else could, suddenly disappeared. It's like being orphaned. I wanted to talk to my dad again. I missed his voice. We kept the answering machine with his last message. I had to feel the pain or get stuck in grief. I worked at Pathways with grieving family members. The healing energy helped fill the emptiness. Fifteen years later, I still wish I could call my dad. I have an antique, black phone sitting next to his photo. When I miss him, I look at his picture and talk to his soul.

I do believe our thoughts travel through the ethers, teleport through time and live on, like the poem Steve Allen wrote when he was seventeen that reached me when I was sixteen, twenty-six years later, just when I needed it. I had an artist friend in the early nineties who told me about a shared vision he had with the mother of a sick child.

Tom had been working for months on a pencil drawing of the face of Christ, wearing the crown of thorns, his pensive eyes looking up to heaven. At the same time, a mother across town was keeping vigil over her dying baby girl, Rita, in need of a liver transplant. Her baby had been ill since she was born.

The day Tom received the first box of prints of his portrait of Christ he turned on the news and saw the story of "Baby Rita." That very day she had received her liver, but the surgeons told her mother the tissue was damaged and it wasn't working. She was weak, and it was unlikely she would survive long enough to get another organ in time. Tom felt an urge to bring his first print of Christ to the baby's mother. He immediately got into his truck and drove to the hospital.

On his way there the baby's mom, Sandy, and her sister went outside of the hospital to a play area and sat on the children's swings, still wet from the morning dew. They prayed one last time for a miracle. Sandy asked God, whatever happened, to watch over her daughter. Then Sandy had a vision of Christ in black-and-white profile, but she could not see his eyes and wished He would turn to face her. A feeling of safety washed over her and she felt her prayers were being answered. When she and her sister returned to intensive care, a nurse handed Sandy a manila envelope. She pulled out the drawing and was in awe. It was the front view of the same face she had seen in her vision. That very hour the failing liver kicked in and her baby's pale face turned a healthy pink. Baby Rita survived.

It took a few years for the mother to track down the artist, but they eventually met and Sandy told Tom about her vision and the impact of his gift. Rumor is that other miracles have occurred through Tom's portrait of Christ. A dad died, a baby lived. Like Rita's mother, sometimes all we can do is pray and surrender.

Always love,

Diana

Chapter 18

Please Don't Squeeze the Shaman or Pull His Finger

Dear Penny,

It is almost Easter, 2013, and I only have about four or five more chapters to write before I finish the story you encouraged me to write. Along my spiritual journey I have met many psychics, gurus and healers. Some of them are only in it for the fame and money, others are deluded and have no real gifts but know how to sell themselves and a few are just crazy. I met one when Bill and I went canoeing in Wisconsin with a group of spiritual seekers. Bill and I, always early, arrived before anyone else and set up our tent. The "spiritual" leader of the group came late and yelled at us for taking the sacred ground he wanted to put up his tent on. An hour later, before we put our canoes in the water, he told me that there was a coil coming out of my head attached to his that was vacuuming up all his knowledge. If I could do that, his head would not be the one I'd syphon. I got away from that guy and avoided him the rest of the trip. Another time I went to a hypnotherapist and sat down in the chair to start. When he asked what I wanted to work on I reminded him I was there for past life regression. The guy said, "Oh, then you need to sit in this seat," and he had me move to a different chair. I never went back to him. Every psychic was not accurate. Sometimes less talented psychics told me wonderful things, like I'd be rich, which hasn't happened. That in some ways was worse than being warned of disaster that I could avoid. Now I can look back and laugh. Most of the practitioners I met were sincere with a desire to help. I have shown how psychics enhanced my life and gave me hope. Never allow a psychic to make important decisions in your life or charge exorbitant amounts of money. I prefer to go to professionals referred by someone.

Sometimes they have waiting lists. Since the 1980s, my teacher Echo Bodine has had readings booked ahead one and a half to two years.

Nurserymates — Diana and Echo at Echo's book signing

I respect the "gifts of the Spirit." They can enhance your life. Just don't give your master your MasterCard. Please don't squeeze the shaman or pull his finger because, like my first publisher and Mr. Coilhead, you'll see just how human they are. That leads me to a real life Shaman.

There is a belief in medicine and healing traditions that what we think affects our health. In medicine it is the "placebo effect," where research documents patients who are given a sugar pill and told they are taking a new drug are "cured." In complementary medicine circles the use of positive affirmations for healing is popular. Scripture teaches that we are made in the image of God, that our thoughts can create reality and like a magnet draw experiences to us, good or bad. I'd say everyone has wished for something improbable and had it come to them unexpectedly. Sometimes it is something insignificant like visualizing a pair of earrings to match a scarf and the exact color and design of earrings shows up at the next store you go to, but sometimes bigger dreams appear.

There were times when I had forgotten I even wanted something and years later it manifested. Below I describe three major events that I never believed would come true.

When I was eight and a child in grade school, wearing a navy school jumper and starched white blouse, I remember sitting at my desk. It had a hole for an ink bottle because we still used fountain pens. The top was marred with kids' names scratched in the wood. I recall the clean smell of a new textbook when I cracked it open and pushed hard on the tight binder to keep it on the page with the map of Egypt. I wanted to go there and see the pyramids and the Sphinx. In the 1990s, I had read *Saved by the Light* and saw the movie about Dannion Brinkley, who was struck by lightning, had a near death experience and woke up psychic. I met him at a Whole Life Expo where he was a motivational speaker. In 2001, Dannion was giving guided tours through the Healing Temples of Egypt. Coincidentally, my friend Mercedes was also a fan of Dannion's and wanted to go to Egypt too. We signed up to go in November. When the planes hit the Twin Towers on 9/11 everything changed. Trips to Egypt were discouraged by the State Department. Like many others, I cancelled the trip, but Dannion called Mercedes and me personally and convinced us to go. The flight was full with Egyptians going home for the holy days of Ramadan. There were few American tourists on that seventeen-hour flight from New York to Cairo.

Our two handsome young guides led us on a vacation of a lifetime. Except for the presence of armed guards, the sites were empty. We freely roamed through the tombs, climbed in the Great Pyramid, took a cruise down the Nile and visited the ancient holy sites. Throughout our stay the sound of men's ritual chanting filled the air, lifting us into a prayerful state. In contrast with the horror of 9/11, the beauty and history of Egypt and the kindness of our guides Yasser and Sarwat, gave me hope.

Diana and Mercedes inside the Great Pyramid in Egypt

My visit emphasized the truth. Muslims are not terrorists. Like in any religion, some teachers distort the spiritual message and indoctrinate children turning them into violent zealots. History shows us that any religion can be hijacked, misrepresenting God, and brainwashing the vulnerable. Religious abuse in all religions is the real enemy we must combat. I was more grateful than ever to live in a country that values religious freedom and separation of church and state. Unfortunately, there are hateful Americans who would prefer to turn back time and live in a country controlled by intolerant fanatics. That is the very mentality that created Isis and feeds it with fear.

The second impossible dream I had when I was sixteen was to visit Steve Allen's house in Encino, California. I knew, because he was an incredibly private man despite his celebrity, this was unlikely to happen.

Diana at Temple of Luxor in Egypt

On October 30, 2000, Bill called me at work to tell me that Steve Allen had died. At first the media reported that he had a heart attack. Later it was confirmed that he was in a car accident. The impact pushed him against the steering wheel. He thought he was okay. Some accounts stated that Steve got out of the car and joked with the driver, "Some people will do anything for an autograph," and drove on to his son's home. There he felt tired and lay down on the sofa where his son could not wake him. The coroner determined the collision damaged his heart causing a slow hemorrhage. I was devastated.

I left work and called the local television stations and told them about Steve Allen saving my life. I did two interviews and wrote a tribute to him that was published in the Star Tribune with a picture of Steve Allen from the Tonight Show. Despite the loss of my book, I finally was able to let people know what a kind man Steve Allen was.

I stayed friends with his wife, Jayne Meadows Allen. Five years later, Jayne called and invited Bill and me to visit her home. We spent five hours talking over tea in their kitchen, sitting in their breakfast nook. Jayne served us appetizers that Steve liked to eat, including smoked salmon, sushi and lemon pound cake. I saw his grand piano where he composed thousands of songs. The house was decorated with valuable artwork including paintings by Toulouse Lautrec, Andy Warhol, Henry Fonda and Al Hirschfeld. Jayne showed us memorabilia from the Tonight Show stored in his office upstairs. There were shelves filled with awards including several Emmys. Some made of cut glass and crystal were lying down to protect them from breaking during an earthquake.

Jayne showed us a large pagoda, a replica of the church in China where Jayne's father served as an Episcopalian minister. Jayne was born in China and lived there until she was seven years old. Her parents were missionaries in danger when the Cultural Revolution began. As they planned to escape from the country, a bomb fell through the roof of their home and landed in the center of their dining room table but never detonated. It was a dud. They moved back to New York, where her mother's family resided, and Jayne was destined to become a glamorous actress and meet Steve Allen. It was an amazing, magical night that we didn't want to end.

The third event that came true was even more impossible. I had read a book about "psychic surgery," an ancient healing tradition that dates back before the time of Christ, where the healer, usually a high priest, can increase his vibrations fast enough to create an opening in the body without making an incision—similar to the way an angel or spirit visitor goes through a wall. Having walked on fire without getting burned, I felt it was a similar mystery where Spirit transcends matter. In the study of Quantum Physics we know that all matter, however dense it appears, is vibrating. The physical world may be the real illusion. These chosen ones are able to raise their frequency to a level that rearranges matter. Sounds like science fiction, but that is the essence of miracles. I believed it was authentic and was so curious I wanted to see it myself, but I didn't have the money to go to South America where it was primarily practiced.

Ten years after I read that book, I was told that a priest from the Philippines who did "psychic surgery" was in Minnesota. Remember, I seldom leave Coon Rapids. A chiropractor invited me to a weekend seminar he was sponsoring for healers to witness and receive the mysterious technique. I had seen skeptics and magicians mimic and fake psychic surgery using props, hidden packets of chicken blood and gizzards, misinforming the public that all of these practitioners were con artists. Of course they never witnessed it or experienced it themselves. They believe in trickery, not miracles. In his book, *Miracles Do Happen—A Physician's Experience with Alternative Medicine*, Dr. C. Norman Shealy, MD describes observing and filming several healers doing "psychic surgery." He collected samples of blood and tissue removed from the procedures and sent them to an independent forensic pathologist and proved the tissue and blood belonged to the patient operated on. It was not from the surgeon or any animal. Of course this is never publicized.

Because blood and tissue are extracted during the "surgery," this practice is not legal in the United States. Ironically, the American Medical Association would prosecute a shaman for "practicing medicine without a license," even though they consider it fictitious. Mysteriously, where these procedures take place without any sterile conditions, infections do not occur, which is attributed to the higher vibrational energy. So rather than reveal his name, because he can see inside the body with x-ray-like vision, I call him God's Eyes.

I had read information about God's Eyes before going to see him. He was raised Catholic, educated by the Jesuits in a private Catholic school. When he was only seven years old he went to the cathedral and an old woman outstretched her hands for help. God's Eyes placed the few coins he had in her palms. She grasped his fingers, looked deep into his eyes and told him he would one day travel to places far away and do wonderful work for the Lord. He was a sickly child who had convulsions and high fevers. As he walked into the church he turned to ask the woman what she meant and she had disappeared. She later came to him in dreams revealing her true identity as Mary, the mother of Christ, reassuring him of his spiritual path. At the age of fourteen, God's Eyes began his healing ministry in the Church of Tzaddi, a nondenominational metaphysical Christian Church.

The day I met him, I was asking for healing for my asthma and the grief of losing my dad and my book. At that time, I happened to have a benign breast lump I'd been getting scanned regularly to watch for changes. I didn't mention it. I was instructed to go into the dressing room, remove all jewelry and clothing and put on a robe. The healing shaman did not charge any set fee for healing but accepted a freewill donation. He had the faith that God would provide him what he needed to survive.

It was a warm summer day and the Filipino priest, who was in his forties, wore jeans and a white T-shirt. There were no sleeves or vestments to hide animal parts or packets of blood in, like the debunkers used. He greeted us with a smile. Looking into his eyes was like staring into the night sky. One client in the reception area told me when he worked on her that his eyes turned from black to sky blue as he took in the Holy Breath. The healing is channeled from Ascended Masters like Christ who are in Spirit. In the corner of the room was a small altar with a statue of baby Jesus the Prince of Peace, holy pictures of saints, a lit white candle, flowers and other blessed objects.

Because I did healing for others, I was allowed to watch him give a healing to another participant before I had my session. The patient reclined on the table. God's Eyes scanned her body, stopping at different areas where he whispered a prayer. His assistant handed her a small transparent glass of clear water for her to hold. He reverently prayed again. I felt the energy shift in the room. His fingers palpated the flesh on her neck. She had thyroid disease. He whispered, "Dear One, think happy thoughts," as his fingers moved rhythmically, palpating the skin. I watched him lift fat, tissue and dark clotted blood from an opening in the neck. He said, "Thank you, Father," and placed the material in the cup of water. He took the cup from her and held it up telling the "patient" to say goodbye. The assistant took the cup of debris and left the room. I watched God's Eyes follow the same ritual as he quickly moved through her body. For a moment a thread-like red line appeared where the spiritual opening had been and then her skin was as it had been before he began.

It was my turn and I hopped up on the table. As he scanned my body he seemed to know every pain in my heart, every shadow in my soul. I felt myself move into a relaxed altered state similar to when I did the firewalk or meditated. Like the woman before me, he palpated my upper right breast and removed something that resembled a yellow lipoma, placed it in the water and said, "Be grateful, Dear One." I had no pain and no sensation of being cut open. I felt a little silly as I said goodbye to the tissue. I thanked Spirit. The next day when I returned he removed more tissue and blood from my fibrocystic breasts. I had three sessions with him that weekend. A few days after returning from the seminar, I felt for the lump and it was gone. There was no scar, no sign of any incision. My husband examined me and agreed. Later I had another mammogram that proved the lump had disappeared. I know that benign tumors often dissolve without any intervention but I had that tumor for over five years. I had become more and more anxious by the monitoring because of breast cancer in my family history.

You are probably wondering if it was so simple why didn't God's Eyes heal my breast cancer when it was discovered years later in my left breast, but he was no longer in the country when I was diagnosed. Believe me, I would have gone to him if he had been here. (After routine surgery I did get healing from a powerful healer I met at Pathways). A few weeks after God's Eyes had gone back to his home country, Bill and I saw the movie *Man in the Moon* about comedian Andy Kaufman's life. The film ended with Kaufman, who was dying from cancer, getting "psychic surgery." When Andy died, the movie inferred that psychic surgery was a scam, but people die from the side effects of radiation and chemotherapy every day yet no one questions that these toxic methods are worth trying. I grabbed Bill's hand. As the theater emptied out, we sat a little longer as the credits rolled. I was extremely aware of the space in my breast where that invasive lump had once been.

I found myself feeling closer to the Spirit of our Christ, the Spiritual Master who predicted others would perform miracles greater than He. He never asked to be worshipped. Christ was a psychic, a channel for the Holy Spirit and above all a

Healer. People who say these powers are evil are denying the Creator's gifts.

I continued to see God's Eyes when he was in town if I felt I needed it. At one point I was having heavy menstruation, uncommon for me, and was concerned. The gynecologist said I had fibroid tumors which was the curse that led to my mother's chronic illness. The priest told me it was normal clotting from menopause and when the results of the ultrasound came back, he was right.

At one point my son wanted to see God's Eyes when he was in town but the healer was booked months ahead. Ken called. The scheduler said he was lucky. God's Eyes just had a cancellation and asked if he could get there in an hour. Ken decided to consult the *Book of Runes* and pull a rune stone from a leather medicine bag I kept in the buffet drawer. Runes are an ancient portent, a Viking oracle that retrieves spiritual advice through your higher self. Ken held the bag of small stones in his hand and asked, "Should I get psychic surgery today?" He pulled out a green blood stone with the symbol of Kano, which means "opening." We were in awe when he read the advice given for that stone:

"This is the Rune of Opening and renewed clarity, of dispelling darkness that has been shrouding some part of your life . . . simply put, if you have been operating in the dark, there is now enough light to see that the patient on the operating table is yourself." The 14th Rune on page 118 was the only page in the book mentioning an operating table.

Not long before Oprah's popular talk show ended, she did a special program on the most famous psychic surgeon, John of God. He takes no credit but claims a group of advanced souls called the Entities take over. One of her producers and an MD traveled to South America to witness the healings that have been practiced for over thirty years in a small village in Central Brazil. He performed healing on the Brazilian President and in gratitude was awarded a Medal of Honor. He has treated millions of people including actress and author Shirley MacLaine, who courageously wrote about taboo subjects like miraculous healing before it was popular. John of God gave healing to spiritual master, Ram Dass, and the famous psychologist/author, Wayne Dyer, whose leukemia was "in remission" after his pilgrimage. On his website and in the book, *John of God — The Brazilian Healer*, you can learn more about this humble man. Not everyone who had a healing was physically healed, but nearly everyone reported being transformed spiritually.

I described three wishes that manifested in my life many years after I had forgotten them. I saw Egypt under extraordinary circumstances, visited Steve Allen's home and visited with his beloved wife Jayne, and had successful spiritual surgery by a psychic surgeon. This is the law of attraction. Our thoughts are powerful. They go out to the Universe and draw people, things and events to us. We are designed to be creators so, as God's Eyes says, "think happy thoughts."

Always love,

Diana

Chapter 19

Conversations with Dog

Dear Penny,

I called Jayne Meadows Allen last week to see how she was doing. She is not well after surgery on her leg, but she answered and we talked for an hour. She was in pain and the meds were not helping. I put her on some healing prayer lists. Miracles have come from the power of prayer.

My sister-in-law told me about a friend who was scheduled for breast cancer surgery. She was placed on a prayer chain at their church and on the day of surgery the lump was no longer there. Doctors sometimes call this "spontaneous remission" but never use the M-word—Miracle. Dr. Larry Dossey, MD, has written several books about prayer and healing showing evidence that patients prayed for do better than patients not prayed for. Well, how about a dog's prayer being answered? There's a successful series of books called *Conversations with God* (Neal Donald Walsh), but I can only admit to conversations with dog. My husband Bill's beloved dog Flicka adored Bill. She wanted to be with him so much that even death could not keep her away.

For over thirteen years, Bill's dog, a dead-grass-colored Chesapeake Bay retriever was his constant companion. The first sign that she was sick was when she was whimpering in pain. Then her back feet dropped under her and she could no longer support her body. The vet confirmed a malignant tumor. It was a terrible morning the day Bill carried Flicka to his truck and laid her in for the last time. I wrote Bill the following tribute for her.

Bill and Flicka on front porch

A Lady's Master

It was the week they weaned me from my mama and put us in a pen that you came down into the dark basement to look at me, my brothers and sisters. I tried to get your attention with my sad, butterscotch eyes. I wagged my tail as hard as I could, pushed my way to you and rubbed my soft, wavy fur against your Red Wing boots. My heart pounded with excitement when you picked me up and held me. My tail beat against your flannel shirt. I licked your hand, hoping you would keep me and not put me back and pick another puppy.

You named me "Flicka," Swedish for Lady. You were my Master. It was wonderful having a home, a rug of my own by the door in the kitchen and a big yard to play in and guard. I loved digging holes in the earth, chewing on branches and rolling on my back in the grass.

You took me to Dog School to teach me not to bite and chew and whine. When I learned, you gave me treats, rubbed behind my ears and played fetch with me. The best time we had was in the autumn when the leaves began to brown on the birch and seeds twirled off the maple. You started to stack your hunting gear in the corner of the basement. I could hardly wait for the morning when I would jump into the back of the truck and settle in for the ride to Gordy's Tree

Farm in Hinckley. You stopped for breakfast and always saved me some bacon and toast.

When you turned into the dirt road by the cabin, I saw Gordy and his dog Sam in the yard waiting. I whined until you let me out. Those were the best times we had, Master, sitting in the wet grass waiting for the ducks to fly over the pond. When you shot a duck, I retrieved it, holding my head high as I swam back to you with the prize. I would sleep hard after a day in the woods, dreaming of the sound of geese, their distant honk echoing across the sky and the succulent smell of grouse cooking on the gas stove.

At home in the winter, when you stoked the fire in the wood-stove, I sat next to your chair while you stroked my warm fur until I fell asleep. In the summer, on the hottest days, you took me down to the Mississippi River and threw a stick into the water, letting me run until I grew tired charging after it.

In my yard, I loved chasing birds and rabbits and watching the night shadows cast by the trees from the light of the campfire you built out back. I watched the flames lick at the wood you cut down at the tree farm after a storm.

I am your Lady Flicka. You are my daily Master—from your first slow footsteps in the kitchen in the morning, to your joyous return from work in the evening to your last gentle touch of my head at night before you went to bed.

I am sorry my eyes clouded over, my body grew tired and stiffened with age and I had to leave you. You had the only key to release me from my pain. You opened the door and let me out, waving goodbye.

I am chasing birds with Sam, warming myself in the sun and still waiting by the Big Door for my Master to come Home.

The next spring, Bill and I went window shopping for furniture. On the way home, as Bill drove by the Vineyard restaurant, he asked me if I wanted to stop for beer and onion rings. I'm sure I gave him a funny look because Bill had never asked me that before. He's not usually spontaneous—more of a methodical planner.

"Sure," I agreed, curious to see what this new man would do next.

As we drove into the parking lot, I saw a woman on

the boulevard behind the restaurant walking a cute, choco-late-brown dog. He looked like he was about six months old. As we headed toward the boulevard, the dog pulled the leash out of the woman's hand and ran directly to us, tail wagging full speed.

"Hi, Puppy. Hi, Boy." I cuddled him behind his ears. "You like that, don't you?" He was friendly.

At first Bill stood back, but the dog jumped at him, insis-tent. Bill stroked his soft, brown fur. "What kind of dog is he?" he asked.

She answered, "I don't really know. He's a mutt, looks part lab. He showed up at our door a year ago, bleeding. I think he was hit by a car. I nursed him back to health. I have a hobby farm in Elk River. I have several dogs so I have to let him go. I'm taking him to the Humane Society in Coon Rap-ids and had just let him out to pee."

"Bill, look, look! He has Flicka's butterscotch eyes. It's a sign." Then the woman said she had watched *Sleepless in Se-attle* the night before and the friends in the movie said every-thing was a sign. Coincidentally, Bill and I had watched the same movie the night before. Bill often teased me about be-lieving in signs. He asked me what the bird shit on my wind-shield meant?

Bill gave me a dirty look. I hadn't even asked him if we could keep him yet. He told me, "I'm not ready for another dog," but then made the fatal mistake of bending down and looking into those soulful eyes. He stood and shook his head.

"We just put our dog to sleep," I explained. I tried to per-suade Bill. "We could try it for a week and take him to the pound if it doesn't work out. Somebody will want him."

"Is he housetrained?" Bill asked.

"Yes, but he's been outside with our other dogs since we got him," she explained. The dog began to tremble. "Oh, he does that when he's nervous. I think he might have been abused by his first owner."

Bill opened the back of his Chevy pickup and lifted the trembling dog into his truck. "What do I owe you?" he asked.

"Nothing. I'm just happy he has a good home. You an-swered my prayers!" She smiled at me. We both knew Bill would never take him to the pound.

Bill asked her about the kind of food he ate, if he'd had his heartworm pills, etc. I never did get my beer and onion rings. As we drove home, I watched the pup in back of the truck. He was still shaking and pacing and didn't like riding. He was small, half the size of Flicka.

"Let's call him Omen!" I said cheerfully.

"Like the horror movie?" Bill snapped.

"No, like the sign. Good Omen!"

"If it doesn't work you are going to take him to the Humane Society, not me."

"I know, I know." I looked out the window and said, "It's your fault. You're the one who had to stop for beer and onion rings."

That night I watched the two of them play outside the kitchen window. I was surprised when Omen went to the back of the yard to poop right where Flicka did her number twos. He followed Bill around the yard. Bill picked up a branch and held it up ready to throw it for the dog to fetch, but Omen hunched and cowered close to the ground, acting fearful as though he'd been hit before. Bill dropped the stick, sat down on the grass and held him, reassuring him that he was safe now. Another odd thing was that Omen didn't bark for a year. The vet told us he had a damaged larynx from being choke-chained by his first owner.

"Good Omen" on rug in kitchen (Flicka's walk in)

That night he stayed in the kitchen on the rug by the door in Flicka's sacred spot. Omen circled and curled up as if he'd been there his entire life. He folded his paw under his foreleg and licked his lower lip just like she did. "You're getting up with him in the middle of the night if he whines," Bill warned as he went to bed, but Omen slept peacefully though the night.

The next morning, I heard Bill open a new package of milk bones and let Omen out through the garage and into the fenced yard, throwing him a treat. By the next week Bill had shortened his name to "O" or, when he didn't obey, "box of rocks."

The next Saturday, when Bill was working overtime, Crystal came over to visit. When she saw Omen she exclaimed, "My God, it's her. Flicka. It's the same energy, in that inferior male body." We both laughed. She held O's face up to hers and looked in his eyes. "You're Flicka, aren't you?"

That evening when Bill came home, I pounced. "Crystal says this is Flicka returned to us." Omen perked up his ears and tilted his head.

"I know," Bill said.

"What do you mean you know?"

"Flicka came to me in a dream last night. She showed me Omen getting dropped off on the highway and getting hit by a car. When the spirit of the dog left its body, Flicka's spirit went in and eventually found her way back to me."

Wow. I was amazed. So Flicka was not reincarnated in Omen as Crystal predicted. She was a walk-in, like the guy in the movie *Heaven Can Wait*. When spirits trade places, one leaves and another takes its place. It gives a whole new meaning to "Walk-Ins Welcome."

Always love,

Diana

Chapter 20

The Holy Molar

Dear Penny,

I love the early spring. Bill and I went to visit your grave site in Anoka. Someone had planted yellow daffodils and purple crocus near your stone. The flowers are just emerging from the wet earth, welcoming the warming sun. Most of the snow has melted except a few stubborn large piles of blackened ice mounds left by the city snowplows.

When I provided healing at Pathways Health Crisis Resource Center, several people who came to me for healing showed me their "new" teeth, telling me they had been to a healing service and seen the visiting evangelist Reverend Willard Fuller. He was an impressive 6'4", in his eighties and looked like a wizard, with long hair and a snow-white beard. He had a healing ministry for decades, with more than 160,000 known testimonials. But he was most famous for dental healings, an ancient form of alchemy, changing decayed and damaged teeth to gold, porcelain and silver described by NASA scientist Daniel W. Fry, Ph.D. in his book, *Can God Fill Teeth?*

A dentist who had examined people who received gold fillings from Reverend Fuller explained that the gold teeth are not implanted teeth but made from molten gold flowing into the cavity, but it is impossible that anyone could tolerate the temperature required to melt gold without having severe burns to their gums or their teeth disintegrating. People who receive the miraculous fillings feel no heat and have no burns. Somehow they are transcended by the healing vibration into an altered state just like a firewalker or the recipient of spiritual surgery. It is another state of consciousness. Is this the key to all healing? Since we can no longer control our environment to avoid polluted air, water, food and electromagnetic fields that cause disease, can we raise our vibration so that we are not affected? Wouldn't it be wonderful to be able to transmute any toxin that enters our body or environment rather than becoming obsessed with everything we ingest? We are bombarded by negative messages that cause immense fear about how unsafe our world is—thoughts sometimes more toxic than the demonized substances themselves.

As more and more people described to me crooked teeth being straightened, crowns being replaced with new teeth, cavities filled and gums healed, I wanted to see Reverend Fuller but I was hesitant because he was an evangelist. Up until that time, I had believed the debunkers who insisted that most revival ministers planted actors in the congregation who pretended to be healed. Reverend Fuller lived in Florida, and I didn't know when he would return to Minnesota. I prayed for guidance asking if I should meet the modern miracle worker. I was impressed by what I had heard of his humility and sense of humor. He called himself the "tooth fairy" and the "holy molar." A sucker for a sense of humor, I was more intrigued than ever and then came synchronicity.

At any given time, I usually have half a dozen books stacked on my night side table, near my bed, waiting to be read. I pulled out a paperback in the middle of the pile that I had purchased at least a year earlier. It was a book of short stories, *He Walks with Me—true encounters with Jesus* by Brad and Sherry Hansen-Steiger. I could read one before I fell asleep. I thumbed through the book when a title caught my eye: *Called to be a Healing Minister When He was Just Fourteen.* A young teenage boy who stuttered was given a message by a stranger that he would be used as a channel for God's work. Because of his speech impediment, the boy, too shy to become a minister, got a degree in Business Administration and Electrical Engineering and joined the U.S. Army.

As I read more about this evangelist, I learned he overcame his stammer and eventually became a Baptist minister. One night his soul was filled with the Holy Spirit and an audible voice informed him he was endowed with the spiritual gifts of miracles and healing. He followed his intuition and began to offer healings and "saw cancers dry up and fall off and goiters disappear." He healed the deaf and the blind and, like in the old tent revivals, people dropped their crutches and walked away, praising the Lord. The conservative Baptist Church he belonged to taught that healing was from the devil. Unable to turn his back on the sick and suffering, the young man was forced to start his own nondenominational healing ministry. The kindly preacher was Revered Willard Fuller, the man I had been praying about.

A few weeks later, the Holy Molar was giving a seminar on the biblical gifts of the Spirit at a hotel in Wisconsin. Sometimes people who came to me for healing questioned if healing was Christian. I thought I might learn something to reassure those who required a Bible reference. The first night, there was a short informational meeting. There I met Ethel, an elderly woman from Illinois who told me she needed $7,000 worth of dental work she could not afford including jaw surgery. Reverend Fuller's hands-on healing had resulted in a straightened jaw and a full mouth of new teeth. Now she and her husband chartered a bus, bringing a dozen people with them to receive healing from the Holy Molar.

The next day I attended the seminar on the biblical gifts of the spirit. The Reverend and his wife Althea were down-to-earth people with a strong faith. They believed they were destined to do healing and that God would provide. Although they charged a minimal fee for teaching their seminars, the healing in the church services was given on a freewill basis. For over forty years they had survived merely on donations. When they passed the basket, several people paid nothing and others who had more money made up for them.

I wished I had that strong a faith and could do just healing full time. As Reverend Fuller described his journey from the hellfire religion of his youth to the progressive mystical Christianity he now taught, I was deeply moved. He believed in everything I did. He acknowledged that reincarnation had been in the original texts of the Bible and had been removed because of power and politics. I was relieved to know this enlightened Evangelist was not afraid of telling the truth and was not channeling healing for the money.

At the first service, I went in the line for healing from his wife Althea. I didn't experience a physical healing for myself, but I met many people who had received healing through both Willard and Althea.

The next day when he spoke, I didn't want the class to end. He taught us each his technique for healing through Jesus Christ and asked that we receive the gifts of the Holy Spirit. One of the gifts he initiated us in was speaking in tongues and I did find myself talking in another language. Having done chanting and repeated mantras in meditation, it did not feel foreign to me. No one translated for me what the words meant, but I believe what was important was that I was lifted into a higher vibration by the sounds, the same way I was when I gave or received a healing. Everything is energy vibrating at a particular frequency. Everything on the Earth plane is a slower, denser frequency, as is disease in the body. Everything in the Spiritual realm is a faster, lighter frequency. The gifts of the Spirit—healing, the gift of prophesy, discerning spirits and speaking in tongues—occur when we raise our vibrations in order to comprehend the Divine. These gifts, like the angels' presence, are made of light, joy and love and are used to give hope and relieve suffering.

At the Sunday night service after the seminar, the church was completely filled. My friend Mercedes met me at the church. She wanted healing for her back pain. She also had a broken tooth that her dentist wanted to pull. We were on the side of the church designated to receive healing from Althea. I went up first and received my healing. Mercedes went next and returned to her seat. She suddenly exclaimed that she felt liquid in her mouth. I looked in and saw liquid silver flowing into the broken tooth. Before my mind could even register what I was seeing, Mercedes had a solid silver filling where the hole had been. I was in awe having witnessed the miracle of alchemy. I kept looking in own my mouth with a mirror and flashlight hoping to see a gold tooth or any sign of dental healing, but I wasn't healed physically that night.

Reverend Willard Fuller and Diana witness a dental healing

One of the participants looked in her own mouth with a mirror searching for gold, and discovered the one silver amalgam filling she had left in a row of white crowns was shaped like a cross. She was so excited she showed everyone who wanted to see. She could start a pilgrimage and charge admission like the woman who had the face of Jesus appear on a charred tortilla, but I think she'd need a lifetime supply of mouthwash and an orthodontist to keep her jaw from locking up.

I later learned that the healing energy continued to work after the prayer service and many people had dental healings, including teeth turning to gold weeks after. Years later my coworker, J. Kay Michelson, needed some dental work and had no dental insurance so I referred her to write Reverend

Fuller care of his ministry *Lively Stones—World Healing Fellowship* in Florida for a distant healing, which is similar to healing prayer. Kay wrote to Reverend Fuller requesting a dental healing. She thanked him ahead of time but sent no money because her husband was out of work and she had none to spare. She wanted relief in particular from a rogue tooth that was growing in the roof of Kay's mouth about an inch back from her front teeth. She received a quick response explaining that Reverend Fuller and a group of healers had immediately sent her healing after reading her letter. A few days later, Kay was sitting in the garage when she felt a sharp movement in her mouth. The stray tooth gently glided back under the skin, turned, moved behind her upper jaw and landed in back of the upper row of teeth. There was no blood, no pain and no scar. She was amazed and shared her experience with me. Most of her teeth were not healed, but the one she asked for was. For some reason several friends who have come to accept my quirky investigations, could not accept the Holy Molar and became quite hostile at the mere mention of his ministry. I understand why, but I no longer doubted the famous and faithful evangelist. I had witnessed and felt the power of healing manifest that night.

Always love,

Diana

Chapter 21

The Healing Super Mother

Dear Penny,

As I became aware that healing sent through prayer, "absent" or "distant" healing was as powerful as when done in person, I met two more powerful healers who practiced what I call "hands-off healing" with amazing results. One was a young mother named Beth.

I met her when I was doing volunteer healing at Pathways. She came to me for relief of migraine headaches. She was a tall, beautiful, young woman with long dark hair and an angelic quality, but she was also a strong, outspoken mother whose abusive marriage was about to end, leaving her as sole caregiver of two sons both born with a rare neuromuscular disease. The boys were on respirators and in wheelchairs, requiring complex 24-hour medical care. If that wasn't stressful enough, Beth discovered after beginning the divorce she was pregnant. She prayed her baby girl would be healthy.

Her sons had survived many invasive medical procedures because Beth was born with the spiritual gifts of psychic intuition and healing that she required to intervene for her children. She had confrontations with medical personnel who made serious errors. Years after I left Pathways, I saw Beth on the news fighting for her sons again. A nursing assistant who watched the boys at night when Beth was sleeping was not giving one of her sons his tube feedings. He became weak with malnutrition and was in grave danger. She had to videotape the negligent employee in order to protect her child and have the worker removed from her home. Beth is the strongest woman I know.

Beth discovered her talents when she was only four years old. She began to see auras, had dreams that would come true and knew things before they happened. She eventually was guided to a teacher who encouraged her to develop her gift of healing. Since then, Beth has worked on thousands of loyal patients. One of the most amazing miracles she facilitated, giving full credit to God, was for a distraught grandmother who called and asked Beth to send "distant" healing to her daughter's baby still in utero. The doctors told the mother her unborn child had spina bifida (an exposed spine) and hydrocephalus (excess fluid on the brain) and was expected to have severe mental impairment and would never walk. Because of the urgency of the situation, Beth sent healing to the fetus at the grandmother's request. When the child was born, the doctors were unable to explain why the spine was enclosed and the extra fluid on the brain was gone. That child can now walk and has no brain damage.

Beth saved another baby who she recognized had RSV, a severe and often fatal respiratory virus. She told the mother to insist the infant be tested. Beth felt an urgency to send "distant" healing to the child and sensed that his life force was leaving and later learned it was at the same time the monitors and alarms went off, signaling the baby was in danger. The baby did have the dangerous RSV virus. Beth continued her silent healing and the infant fully recovered and was soon sent home.

I believe that, along with the protective instincts of motherhood, the gift of healing, as part of nature, is given to all mothers to nurture and heal their infants when they are most vulnerable. Mothers are often healing their babies with touch without even knowing it. Women also become more psychic with motherhood. There are abundant stories of mothers having premonitions when their children are sick or in danger, motivating them to seek medical attention often before the symptoms are obvious. I hope that more mothers learn about the spiritual gift of healing so they can help their children and their families. I wish I had known about energy healing when my son was a baby.

Beth encouraged my healing work and told me that I needed to do more. Beth was the healer I chose to send me "distant" healing when I had breast cancer. As a medical intuitive, she gave me reassurance that I could never receive from a medical doctor who believed I was only "in remission."

Beth's baby girl was born without the neurological disease. Her intelligent sons are thriving and now attending college classes. Beth now has a healing practice in her home, providing numerous forms of energy work to her clients (Qigong, bioenergy, craniosacral therapy, myofascial release, hands-on healing and distant healing).

I have met many wonderful healers, but I will never forget the strength of the healing super mother and the Holy Molar. The miraculous nature of such dramatic physical healings where tumors disappear, teeth grow, jaws are rearranged and diseases vanish is similar to the healing that occurred to a girl from Mississippi named Cheryl Prewitt, described in her book *A Bright and Shiny Place*. Her leg was crushed in a childhood accident, leaving her with pain, severe scarring and one leg two inches shorter than the other. Her limp was so bad she was teased and bullied in school. In a series of Divine Interventions, Cheryl's leg was gradually healed, culminating at a prayer service where her leg instantaneously grew two inches. All signs of her injury, including the ugly scars, were gone. She grew up to become Miss America 1980.

Always love,

Diana

Photo of Beth Bauer and family
Front Row: Alex, Levi
Back Row: Max, Amanda, Isabella, Beth and Fiancé Scott

Chapter 22

No Place Like OM

Dear Penny,

This chapter is written in memory of Natasha Whaalen, an acupuncturist I went to for treatment. She loved Chinese Medicine. I know she lived in Anoka, Minnesota, a few blocks from you, Penny. I had a call into Natasha to set up another appointment but never heard from her again. On September 19, 2008, I was watching the news and saw a horrific story about a woman who was murdered; her body was placed on her motorcycle and pushed off the road in an effort to stage an accident. It was Natasha.

She'd been killed, leaving her then five-year-old daughter without a mother. Her boyfriend, the father of their child, and his brother were later convicted. It was reported drugs were involved and their sentences were too lenient.

Natasha had shared with me that she'd hoped to leave the relationship but couldn't afford to until her business increased. She was a beautiful tall blonde with exotic green eyes. I wondered why someone so stunning had so little confidence and seemed so sad. She was proud that she had become a licensed acupuncturist and very excited about her work. I had hoped she could get out of that relationship. I had no idea she was in danger. I wonder if she was trying to leave the morning she was killed in the garage. Of course her death brought back the horror of my own escape from domestic abuse and being involved with a man who became a murderer. If only Natasha had escaped. I again relived the survival guilt I had when Susan Marek was killed. Where were the angels then? The irony is not lost on me.

Before I met Natasha the acupuncturist, I already knew the value of acupuncture from my friend Mercedes Summers.

She had helped my son, Ken. He had a calcified stone in his bile duct, blocking the salivary gland. It hurt every time he swallowed. The tissue around the stone had swelled to the size of a golf ball. On his doctor's advice, he sucked on lemon drops and massaged the area in an effort to move or dissolve it, which sometimes works, but it didn't help him. Eventually he had a procedure to remove the stone. Unfortunately, in an effort to grasp it with a wire, the doctor pushed it further back down the bile duct and could not retrieve it. Kenny was scheduled for surgery and was warned there was a risk that the left side of his face could be permanently paralyzed with the procedure. At that time, Mercedes, a nurse who had just received her Master's degree in Oriental Medicine and acupuncture, offered to help. The week before Ken's scheduled surgery, she did acupuncture with electrodes attached to the needles. The next day, Kenny called me and said he was coming right over to show me something. He explained he had gone to the Emergency Room with excruciating pain. While he was lying on the cot behind a curtain, he felt something moving under his chin that dropped below his tongue. He reached into his mouth and picked out the stone. It was the size of a Tic-Tac mint, but three times the size of the duct. The pain had stopped. Ken no longer required the potentially disfiguring surgery. I was so relieved.

Acupuncture has been practiced in China for thousands of years. It is not just used for pain. It is commonly used to treat breech babies. Often, after only one to three sessions, the infant will turn around into the correct birthing position. I was intrigued with Chinese Medicine because it was based on moving energy, like the hands-on healing I do. I was also upset that Western Medicine not only ignores a simple procedure that could save babies' lives, it often scoffs at anything not taught in medical school. I worked with a woman whose uncle had been hiccupping continually for three years and nothing he tried to stop it worked. There have been cases of people hiccupping for more than twenty years. I told her I knew that acupuncture was a treatment used for hiccups. Her uncle tried it and after three sessions his hiccups stopped. People today in China routinely receive treatment with Chinese and Western Medicine, respecting both modalities. Maybe someday we will advance enough to use everything available to heal us.

Back to the present; Penny, the house next door is for sale. I think it is a foreclosure. There are several empty homes in the neighborhood since the real estate bubble burst. This morning a young couple knocked on our door. They were interested in buying the neighboring house and asked about the trains that run on the track behind our yard. The Amtrak, the new North Star commuter and freight trains speed through on a regular basis. I told them after being here for thirty years I don't really hear the trains anymore.

It was a train that indirectly led me to the next healer I would meet, a Chinese Qigong Master. As I pulled up to the safety arm at the railroad crossing one morning on my way to work, the woman behind me in a green truck put on her brakes too late and rear-ended me. Had she not stopped, I'd have been pushed into the path of the train. When I got out of the car, she said, "I didn't think you were going to stop." The arm was down! Where else was I going? I felt nauseous and lightheaded and by the end of the week was in severe pain with a serious whiplash injury, triggering my old fear of driving. I found a chiropractor covered by my auto insurance. Adjustments and massages were helpful for back pain, but the compression of my chest exacerbated my asthma so I kept searching for a healer that was right for me.

While I was still volunteering at Pathways giving healings, I met a woman who told me about a healer who cured her asthma without even touching her. He stood a foot away from the chair she sat in and moved energy. She had thrown away her inhalers. I had heard of the Qigong Master before but assumed he was farther away than I wanted to drive, but she told me that he lived in Coon Rapids. Master Lin taught Spring Forest Qigong at the local community college fewer than two miles from my house. I signed up to take his first level Qigong class, hoping he could help me.

Qigong Master Chunyi Lin was born in China and followed a remarkable path that led him to Minnesota. During the Cultural Revolution, the ancient practice of Qigong healing was outlawed and practitioners were forbidden to practice it to heal themselves or others. This made Master Lin's journey, described in the book *Born a Healer* by Master Chunyi Lin and Gary Rebstock, even more miraculous.

Anyone who owned property or livestock, was a landlord or educated was considered an enemy of the state. Master Lin's family was targeted by soldiers because his father was the manager of a salt company. His uncle was buried alive up to his neck and shot in the head because he had owned a water buffalo twenty years earlier. Suddenly friends became spies for the government. They lied and turned people in to protect themselves and their families. His father was imprisoned and his mother fled into hiding, leaving her four children alone with an elderly nanny. Former friends turned on the family and forced the children and old woman into the streets. They were separated and followed an elaborate plan of escape. While Chunyi and his sister were on the run, two armed soldiers stopped them. Recognizing who they were, one of the men said he would kill them. He placed a machine gun to the nine-year-old boy's head, but the other soldier convinced the man to let them go. There were several close calls for Chunyi Lin, with a boat ride over stormy seas, manual labor, poisonous snakes and being near starvation, but he survived. Eventually, Master Lin reunited with his parents. They were still considered outcasts, but in a series of uncanny events he received a college education and became a professor at Zhaoging Institute.

While playing basketball, Chunyi Lin had a serious sport's injury. During a jump shot, in an effort to avoid landing on a fallen player's chest, he twisted his legs sideways. When he landed, both his knees shattered. He was unable to walk and lived in severe pain. In desperation, he went to see a visiting Qigong Master with thousands of others at a stadium, where the practitioner sent healing energy to the crowd for seven hours. Chunyi Lin's physical healing began that day. He was determined to study this powerful technique. His spirit was wounded by the atrocities he had seen, but the Qigong movements gradually lifted him out of grief, allowing him to forgive and trust again.

Qigong healing had given Chunyi Lin his life back. He was a disciplined student but was not satisfied to just heal himself. He wanted to help others who were suffering. The old Qigong Masters refused to teach him this, saying he was not ready. They told him it might take decades, or lifetimes, before he was allowed to learn the secret. It was similar to the movie *Dragon*, the Bruce Lee story where Lee was brutally attacked for breaking the taboo against teaching hidden martial arts.

Eventually, during years of strict fasting, Qigong practice and long hours of meditation, like angels, Spiritual Masters came in spirit to Chunyi Lin, showing him how to heal the sick and imploring him to teach others how to heal themselves. With incredible serendipity, the young professor landed in Coon Rapids, Minnesota, teaching Chinese language and culture. He later was invited to teach a simple form of Qigong, in a community education class he designed for people who were recovering from illness. Few people had ever heard of Qigong. Five people showed up, three by mistake.

There he met Esther Trejo, a woman wheeling an oxygen tank, who was left at the class by her son and reluctant to believe that anything could help her. She was in the end stage of villiary proteinosis, a rare lung disease requiring a heart/lung transplant, and had no interest in Qigong. Eight weeks later, after she began doing the movements and received healing in class by Master Lin, Esther was off oxygen, walking, with no sign of the disease. (You can see Esther's moving testimonial on the Spring Forest Qigong website.) Esther and Chunyi Lin became friends. Generously sharing her story, she inspired many people to become students of Qigong. After training thousands of students and several Qigong masters, Chunyi Lin has become internationally acclaimed and opened the Spring Forest Qigong Center in Eden Prairie, Minnesota.

The power of spiritual healing in most traditions and religions has been shrouded in mystery and reserved for male priests, shamans and masters, until now. Religions that hijacked Christianity, saying they were the only ones with the truth, tortured and burned medicine women, prophets and healers because their power threatened the status quo. That is how these original, natural gifts from God became known as the "occult," which really means hidden, not evil. Christ Himself invited everyone, including women, to do healing. It was the sexism and politics of the times that forced practitioners to go underground.

Qigong movements open blockages of energy, allowing it to flow again, facilitating healing. Western Medicine treats symptoms, targeting separate organs, often requiring permanent dependence on prescription drugs and/or surgery. Chinese Medicine treats the whole body with the goal of permanent healing, not just maintenance of the disease. It has worked for thousands of years, for millions of people who rely on Qigong practice to keep them healthy.

In Master Lin's classes, I heard amazing stories of healing, many described in his book. I had taken all four levels of Spring Forest Qigong. I even heard about a student with late stage HIV/AIDS who was too weak to perform the physical Qigong movements who used Master Lin's guided meditation tapes to move the energy, receive healings and slowly regain his health. The last I heard, he had tested negative for the next ten years. Of course Western Medicine would say he was only "in remission."

Master Lin's meditation CDs helped lift my spirits when I was diagnosed with cancer. When I practice the active Spring Forest Qigong movements, I sometimes feel my soul move into a sacred space where I am dancing with God. That is the goal of spiritual practice: to become conscious of Spirit. It is not about "earning heaven" but being aware of the ever-present Divine. I have only had glimpses of awareness through Qigong, meditation, prayer and while giving and receiving healing, but there are enlightened souls that never lose sight of God.

Regardless of one's beliefs or spiritual practice, it is a difficult time to be on earth now with the heavy energy of fear and violence, without becoming discouraged. It has helped me to know that we have more spiritual knowledge available than ever before to help us cope.

There are people alive who are enlightened and have reached permanent realization of God. They anchor the Light and protect us from ourselves. Their presence raises us up.

Many Spiritual Masters on the "other side," too numerous to name them all—like Jesus, Krishna, Buddha, Mohammed, Yogananda, Mother Mary, Kwan Yin, saints, angels and unnamed benefactors—are a constant Source of Light waiting to intervene. We can call on them for assistance any time.

What I loved most about Spring Forest Qigong is that you do not have to pay to see a healer but can learn with practice to heal yourself and others. I admit I was not very diligent in practicing Qigong and my asthma was not completely healed, but Spring Forest Qigong increased my faith in all healing. Although I still use preventative bronchodilators, I have not had an asthma attack for over seven years and no longer have had to go to the emergency room. There was another reason I was meant to meet Chunyi Lin: the Qigong Master helped my son.

Ken had ulcerative colitis—a genetic "gift" from his estranged father. It became so serious he was unable to stop the bleeding. He had to take a medical leave of absence from work, eventually losing his job, his medical coverage, his girlfriend and his house. He tried a common prescription drug prescribed for colitis and had an allergic reaction, ending up in urgent care. His head swelled, he had pressure on his chest, could not breathe and could have gone into anaphylactic shock and died. Unable to take prescription medication, his only option was to try natural remedies and healers. Most people do not seek these methods until medicine has failed them and they are in serious trouble, making it even more amazing when a miracle occurs.

I gave him healings and he received treatment from Beth, but he was not getting better, so I advised him to see Master Lin. After the very first healing session, the bleeding stopped. In total he had only three appointments with Master Chunyi Lin and the colitis was gone. Thirteen years later, he still has not had another episode of ulcerative colitis. His illness increased his compassion for others. Since then, Ken has used Qigong healing to relieve pain for his friends and their pets.

I have seen too many miracles not to believe in healing. Without leaving Minnesota, I met many wonderful healing facilitators and highlighted the seven who renewed my faith:

Steven Sonmore, Echo Bodine, God's Eyes, Reverend Willard Fuller, Beth Bauer, Mercedes Summers and Master Chunyi Lin.

It is encouraging to know that miracles are not reserved for the distant, dusty past but are happening all around us, in all countries through many faiths. Like prayer, it unites us. The Creator does not care what religion you are or what name you call God. Healing is a sacred gift of nature available to everyone to enhance their lives. My hope is that Master Lin's trademark motto comes true: "A healer in every family and a world without pain."

Always love,

Diana

Qigong Master Chunyi Lin and Diana (He healed her son)

Chapter 23

Got Off My "But"

Dear Penny,

So, my "butterfly sister," I finally finished the book. In the first chapter, I wrote about the summer we both miraculously experienced a butterfly land on our breast cancer sites.

After you passed over, your spirit showed up in a psychic reading and you told me you'd "kick my butt" if I didn't start writing another book. I quit making excuses and got off my big but—**BUT** after losing the book and movie rights to my first book and, after writing other book manuscripts that no one has ever read, why would I start over? I still wanted to give people hope the way Steve Allen's book had given me.

As the years flew by, the synchronicity kept coming. Bill and I went to a bed and breakfast in Duluth, Minnesota with a gift certificate from my son. There was a grand piano in the front room of the old mansion that played music and, like the old player pianos, the keys moved. There were only a few discs available. When I looked through them, I was stunned to find one of Steve Allen's music with the song he had composed for his television show, "This Could Be the Start of Something Big."

A few weeks ago I talked to his wife, Jayne Meadows Allen. She is almost ninety-six years old. I was surprised when she answered the phone. Usually her caregivers pick it up since she has been ill and confined to her bedroom. We talked for an hour. She, as always, had many wonderful stories about Hollywood to share. Last fall, after she fell and broke her wrist and shoulder, she could no longer write in long hand. That was when she called and gave me her home phone number. She thanked me for her birthday gift and told me proudly that flowers had just been delivered that were sent from Jay Leno. (It is Bill's fantasy to visit Jay Leno's garage and see his extensive collection of classic cars.) Jayne still received fan mail from around the world. I had always looked forward to her letters and have over forty in Jayne's beautiful handwriting. She is known for her glamour and acting talent, but few people know how intuitive and sensitive she is. When we talk on the phone, I always hate saying goodbye, unsure if it will be the last time we talk.

As I did the last rewrite of this chapter, I received a call from my sister-in-law telling me that Jayne had passed away on Saturday, April 26, 2015, at her home in Encino. I felt sad to lose such a wonderful friend and relieved that she had been released from her pain and reunited with her beloved Steve. There were many beautiful YouTube videos online giving tribute to Jayne, describing her career in Broadway, the movies and television. In one video, showing an interview with both Steve and Jayne, she said to the talk show host, "There is nothing Steve could do that would make me divorce him." Steve immediately quipped, "Now she tells me!" They were Hollywood Icons and a loving couple who made you believe in soulmates.

So, Penny, I realize now my religious indoctrination was from the less-than enlightened who taught me that God wanted me to suffer because we are born wicked and unworthy. Believing everything they taught, I didn't need enemies. I sabotaged myself. Like a magnet, my thoughts attracted suffering. Heaven's angels kept me alive, but many earth angels, like Steve Allen and Reverend Eve Olson, gave me hope. When I changed the fearful thoughts from my "given" religion to thoughts that God had breathed in me, that I deserved to survive, to find love and joy, my life changed forever. I was guided by the unseen and given my son, my wonderful husband, the gift of healing, and the witness of miracles. I inherited my mother's shame and suffering from her vows of silence. I hope, in being honest, I released some of her tortured thoughts from the abuse she suffered, and honored her memory.

Of the thousands of healings I have done, two for my family stand out. My son, Ken, had surgery on his shoulder to repair a sports injury. Bill and I made a treacherous trip to Unity Hospital in a winter storm. The streets and power lines were coated with ice. I stopped in the gift shop and bought Kenny a large, heart-shaped, red balloon. When we entered the room he was alone. No other relatives or friends had called or visited. He told me he was in excruciating pain and the prescription drugs were not helping. I gave him a short hands-on-healing, and he fell asleep. The next day he called. "Mom, after the healing, the pain was gone." I was grateful I had learned about healing energy. I hope more parents will learn to ask for healing and a new generation of healers will help their children.

Diana and Ken

Bill and Ken

The second experience channeling healing energy that I am especially grateful for was for my beloved husband Bill. He was diagnosed with prostate cancer in 2005. We were told he did not have the usual slow-growing form of prostate cancer but had a "fast-growing," more deadly form. The summer he had his surgery, I was unexpectedly laid off from my job as a medical transcriptionist, a blessing because Bill had complications from surgery and needed my help during his recovery. I cried every day that summer, fearful of losing my husband and wondering if I would ever find another transcription job because they are becoming obsolete. The work is being sent overseas, transcribed by doctors themselves, or employees are switching to voice recognition or scribes.

Bill had radiation treatment following the surgery. He has also taken testosterone blockers for many years, because the hormone is believed to feed prostate cancer. He tolerates the side effects, but I have to stop him from redecorating the house. I was able to give Bill an energy healing every day for three months, over ninety healings. I also put his name on many prayer lists. He had three healings from Master Lin. It has been ten years since he was diagnosed with cancer and there is no recurrence. You may think healing doesn't exist, but our wonderful bodies are continually healing us. At the end of that summer, I accepted a new medical transcription job, where I have now worked for ten years.

When I was diagnosed with Stage 2 breast cancer, I had a lumpectomy to remove the malignant tumor. It had not spread to the margins or the lymph nodes. After working in the medical field as a transcriptionist for 35 years and doing healing with cancer patients for over twenty years, I made the opposite choice most people make. I decided not to get radiation, chemotherapy or to take estrogen-blocking drugs. It was a crap shoot. As your body ages you are often faced with a situation where you pick your poison—when you have to decide whether the drug or intervention is riskier than the disease. I chose instead to receive "distant" energy healing from Beth. I was also on several prayer chains and received one healing from Master Lin. I have been "cancer free" for six years. I would never recommend what I did to others. I was in a unique place to accept the consequences. Bill and I survived against the predicted medical statistics. I respect medicine. I know I would have died without asthma inhalers or antibiotics. I also believe energy healing gave my husband and me more time to be together, regardless of what happens in the future.

Diana and Bill together thirty-five years

Not everyone who gets healing is healed, nor does everyone who receives medical treatment get cured, but the Creator has given us both wonders, medical science and spiritual energy that abounds in nature, to ease our agony. Long before modern medicine existed, which is only a few hundred years old, our souls remembered coming from God and knew how to tap into the Light for good. We are awakening again to what we have always known. Both medical science and spiritual healing can enhance our lives.

Hoping for another miraculous healing for the last chapter, I found more. Many years ago, I read an article about a woman who tried for years to get pregnant and had given up when she went to a sacred site and prayed to have a baby, even though she knew it was medically doubtful she could conceive. It was at the Santuario de Chimayo in New Mexico, located above Santa Fe. Shortly after the woman returned home, she and her husband learned they would finally be having their first child. Bill and I recently traveled to the church where miracles have manifested since 1810. That was the year Bernardo Abeyea found a crucifix buried in the sand. He dug it up and brought it to the local priest who was miles away, but more than once the crucifix disappeared and was rediscovered again on the spot where it was first found. Long before the cross was first uncovered, the land was considered sacred by the Native Americans.

Unable to remove the crucifix from the holy site, the Catholic priest had a small adobe church built in Chimayo. Since then, pilgrims have come to collect the "holy dirt" from the room called the "pocito" or well, searching for spiritual, emotional and physical healing.

The first night in Santa Fe, I did have altitude sickness and felt like I was dying. I was lightheaded, anxious, fatigued and more short-of-breath than usual. That evening we went to a restaurant called Upper Crust Pizza, sat on the patio and ordered an artisan pie and two margaritas. We were surprised to learn that the high altitude makes alcohol more potent. They were the best margaritas we ever had and helped us adjust to the new climate.

On Sunday, we arrived early at the sanctuary when it

opened. Once inside, we walked to the left where there were two small rooms. We entered the first, where crutches left from the healed and photos of petitioners requesting miracles hung on the adobe walls. There were long wooden benches to sit on and wait your turn to go into the second smaller room. When the family inside came out, Bill and I ducked our heads down to enter through the low doorway. The approximately 6' x 6' space was nearly bare except for a few Christian artifacts that hung on the wall, preserved under glass. The light brown stone floor had a hole in the center filled with sand that sparkled with occasional bits of crystal. A scoop was provided. Bill had purchased four small round containers. I filled them with sand, stepped aside and prayed for my family and friends. I felt my mom was happy that I had entered a Catholic Church. I was more at peace with my past. Although I could never be Catholic again, I could forgive the abuse, be less afraid of religious zealots, and respect others for their beliefs, while cherishing my own hard-won faith. Bill and I felt power and grace in that sacred place, similar to what we felt when we visited the energy vortexes in Sedona, Arizona.

When I arrived home, I read more testimonials. The most dramatic account was about a young man who had friends bring him back "holy dirt" from Chimayo. They also asked the priest to say a Mass for him once a month for a year asking God to heal his renal cancer. He spread the dirt over his abdomen. Shortly after, the cancer disappeared and never returned. That was nineteen years ago. He later converted to Catholicism.

The experience reminded me of a Hindu swami who manifested holy ashes and objects from thin air. He is now in Spirit. I was blessed to have a friend whose relative went on a pilgrimage from Nepal to India and ended up at the yogi's ashram. When the mystic passed through the crowd, where the mother was praying for her grown daughter, he looked directly into her eyes and nodded his head in recognition. A few months later the mother was thrilled to learn that her child had quit using drugs and alcohol, and was healed of a serious, debilitating addiction. She has been "clean" for nearly twenty years. Her mother believes the guru granted her wish.

Like other yogis, he materialized sacred ash called "vibhuti," known to have healing properties. My friend gave me a small container of vibhuti. A few months ago, I shared some of the ashes with another friend who, during a pelvic exam, was told she had a hard lump in her uterus. She went home and spread the ashes over her pelvis, praying for a miracle. The next week she went in for imaging. Two weeks later, when she went back to the clinic for the results of the ultrasound, the bewildered physician told her there was no longer any visible mass. My friend just smiled, not sharing that she believed she was healed. There are many accounts of devotees who shared their vibhuti with others, whose empty containers of ash were mysteriously replenished.

The miracles I have shared in this book are only a few examples I learned about from my little domain in Coon Rapids, Minnesota, leading me to believe that healings, usually kept secret, occur every day, in every culture, and religion around the world. Obviously, we are not healed to live forever in our bodies, but to be here long enough to do what we are divinely brought here to accomplish. That mission is unique to everyone. We do not consciously remember, but our soul carries the blueprint.

When I was visiting my twin sister Donna on Thanksgiving a few years ago, she had a surprise for me. I was invited to the house next door to meet her neighbor, Nesta, who shared my love for the supernatural. Nesta told me that she was the daughter of Eve Olson, the spiritualist minister and medium who helped me after I miscarried. She was there after my boyfriend, the father, was convicted of murdering Susan Marek on the playground where I had conceived. Eve saw me having a better future. She helped me through the survival guilt, renewed my faith and guided me through the years of domestic abuse. Nesta opened the glass curio cabinet door. Inside was her mother's collection of angels. She took out a tiny, white porcelain angel playing a cello and placed it in my hand, saying, "The spirit of my mother wants you to have this." When I got home I looked closer at my gift, seeing the little angel had a broken wing. Part of it had been glued back together. It had been damaged and mended, and so had I. I placed it on a shelf in my office, in front of the few copies I had left of my first book, near the framed photo of me and Steve Allen smiling on the day we met.

The angels coerced me back from heaven and kept their promise to protect me from rape, suicide, murder, a violent psychotic ex-husband, religious abuse, psychiatric misdiagnosis, threatening legal battles and cancer. I kept my promise to tell the truth. I found out what truth to tell: the misrepresentation of God, the power of changing your beliefs and the gift of healing. Although I may not have convinced you to believe, I am sure we are here, sceptic and faithful alike, to anchor the Light. This true story is written to give hope, in return for the *Promise of Angels.*

I have to leave, Penny. The sun is setting. Bill and I are going on the Ghosts of Anoka Tour in your neighborhood. I have a feeling you will be joining us.

Always love,

Diana

Religious abuse is the misrepresentation of God with false beliefs that immobilize us with fear and guilt. We become trapped in our belief of unworthiness and attract suffering. Listed below are common abusive religious beliefs that insult God and encourage self-hatred, violence and war. Life-enhancing beliefs trust God, nurture our Divine nature and attract hope, love, joy and healing.

Abusive Religious Beliefs	Life-Enhancing Spiritual Beliefs
1) Religion and God are the same.	Religion was manmade in the dark ages. God is Spirit.
2) Religion talks about God.	Spirituality is awareness of God so acts in accordance.
3) I am a sinner.	God has breathed Divine life into me. I am good.
4) I am not worthy.	I deserve life, love and joy.
5) Suffering is the way to heaven.	Joy is the celebration of God. Heaven is home.
6) We must guard against evil.	We are protected by angels and God's Light.
7) God judges us.	We judge our lives after death in higher consciousness.
8) The Bible is the only knowledge of God.	God is not only contained in one book but in our DNA.
9) The clergy knows best.	God is best known within our soul, a holy template.
10) Fear is necessary.	Fear is the absence of faith and attracts chaos.

11) God created Hell to punish us.

Hell is a human creation, on earth, and the astral plane.

12) Only Jesus heals.

Healing is God's gift of nature for all, like the air and sun.

13) There is only one way to God.

There are many paths that lead to the Source.

14) Psychics are evil.

Intuition is the gift we were all given to hear God.

15) We must fear death.

There is no death, only leaving the body to go home.

16) Healing works only if you believe.

Belief is not required. Animals, babies and plants heal.

17) We can't pick and choose beliefs.

All scripture has been edited. Free will chooses.

18) God wants worship.

Needing praise is a projection from the ego of man.

19) What religion you belong to matters.

We are all one with God, regardless of religion.

20) Being LGBT is an abomination.

We are all souls, not bodies. All Love matters.

21) Women must be controlled by men.

Souls being Divine are all equal.

22) God does not forgive all sins.

God sees our Divinity and nothing to forgive.

23) I'm saved, you are not.

We were never lost. It's not a competition.

24) You're going to Hell if you don't believe in God.	We all forget God at times. It's human.
25) Revenge is justified by others' sin.	Revenge endorses endless hate and never wins.
26) The paranormal is satanic.	All sacred texts are filled with supernatural wonders.
27) My religion is the only true one.	A vain deceit that keeps you from thinking or leaving abuse.
28) Animals have no souls, no heaven.	All living creatures are filled with Divinity and own eternity.
29) Reincarnation is not true.	God gives us many chances; some were born yesterday.
30) We know God by studying scripture.	Yes, but the mind cannot hold God, only the soul.
31) We have to earn Heaven.	Heaven is our Home where we come from and will return.
32) Abortion is murder.	The soul survives in heaven, is conceived by another mother or the same mother at a better or safer time. Planning parenthood and providing contraception prevents abortion more than judgmental religions do.

Acknowledgements

Telling this true story has been my obsession, and I am grateful to many people who have inspired me along the way to never quit, especially:

My wonderful son, Ken, who always encouraged my healing work and writing. He listened to endless rewrites until they felt complete. My beloved husband, Bill, who makes me feel loved, safe and cherished.

Thanks to my family and friends for their encouragement and love. To Darlene Hauff, a friend who never stopped telling me that writing is a gift I must not waste.

In memory of Steve Allen—Hollywood Icon and the first host of the *Tonight Show*—who saved my life when I was a suicidal teenager and began a lifetime of correspondence. He was my mentor in this life and watches over me from the next. To Jayne Meadows-Allen—Steve's wife, a glamorous movie star, a sensitive friend. I miss her beautiful handwriting and her unique voice.

In memory of my friend, Penny, who passed over in 2011. (Name changed at request of family.) We had cancer at the same time. She encouraged my writing and healing work. This book is written in the form of letters to Penny, my "butterfly sister."

To my current coworkers and all medical transcriptionists, hidden professionals who make sure medical records are accurate. They are independent, intelligent and patient. After doing this work for decades, many of my dearest friends are transcriptionists.

My son and I were blessed to survive domestic abuse. To the memory of Susan Marek and Natasha Whaalen, both murdered by violent men. In memory of veteran Michael Casey, my first love, who died from leukemia, caused by exposure to Agent Orange in Vietnam. One day, when we all truly honor the Divine in everyone, war and violence will end.

I write in memory of author Emily Crofford, my first writing teacher. I thank all the writers who have listened to me read in support groups over the years, especially those from Quillmasters—a group I was in for over fifteen years—and more recently the writers' support group at The First Congregational United Church of Christ in Anoka. Writing saved my life. I believe writing can heal our wounds, even if it does not reach others.

I am grateful to all the healers, psychics and mediums who connected me with angels and Sacred Spirit, giving me hope when I needed it most. Thanks to my friends from Unity North Spiritual Center for their generous insights and encouragement. Thanks to the most influential "Lightworkers," whose stories are in the book. They have enhanced my life and at times saved it.

To Jansina, from Rivershore Books, for her professional and kind guidance helping me self-publish *Promise of Angels.* She is an editor with generosity and heart. I admire her intelligence and courage to pursue publishing with integrity in an often cutthroat business.

Thank you to the Edge Magazine, publishers Tim Miejan and Cathy Jacobsen. You don't know me, but your publication affected my healing journey since 1996 with profound synchronicity. Many of the practitioners who advertise in your holistic living magazine showed up in my life right when I needed them. I have found no other spiritual resource as valuable.

Thanks to Jim Roach, MD, author of *God's House Calls: Finding God Through My Patients,* for taking the time to write the foreword. I am thrilled such a wonderful doctor understood my intention to give others hope and honored me with his kind words.

Thanks to anyone taking time out of their busy lives to read *Promise of Angels* and help me keep my promise.

Bibliography

Allen, Steve. *Bop Fables*, Simon and Schuster, 1955.

Allen, Steve. *Mark it and Strike It*, Holt, Reinhart and Winston, 1960.

Allen, Steve. *Princess Snip-Snip and the Puppykittens*, Platt and Monk, 1973.

Allen, Steve. *Beloved Son: A Story of the Jesus Cults*, Roberts-Merrill, 1982.

Bible, The Gideons, King James version. 1 Corinthians 12:4-11, 12:10-12:13, Romans 12: 6-8. (In reference to the gifts of the Spirit).

Blum, Ralph H., *The Book of Runes*, Thomas Dunne Books, 2008.

Bodine, Echo. *Hands That Heal*, New World Library, 2004. HarperOne, 2008.

Brinkley, Dannion. *Saved by the Light*, HarperOne, 2008.

Cumming, Heather and Leffler, Karen, *John of God: The Brazilian Healer Who Touched the Lives of Millions*, Atria Books/ Beyond Words. 2007. (Featured on The Oprah Winfrey Show. See on You-Tube).

Dossey, Larry, M.D., *Healing Words: The Power of Prayer and the Practice of Medicine*, HarperOne, 1995.

Fry, Daniel W., Ph.D., NASA Space Scientist, *Can God Fill Teeth*, Self-Published, 1970.

Hathaway, Stark R, PhD and McKinley, J.C., MD, University of Minnesota, *MMPI (Minnesota Multiphasic Personality Inventory)*, 1942.

Lerma, John, M.D., *Into the Light*, New Page Books, 2007.

Lin, Chunyi and Rebstock, Gary, *Born a Healer*, Self-Published 2002, Limited Edition.

McEneaney, Bonnie, *Messages: Signs, Visits and Premonitions from Loved Ones Lost on 9/11*, William Morrow, Imprint of Harper Collins Publishers, 2010.

Michael, Diana Louise, *Name of book withheld for my protection*, 1993 (Out of Print).

Prewitt-Salem and Slattery, Kathryn, *A Bright and Shiny Place*, Praise Books, 1987.

Roach, Jim, MD, *God's House Calls: Finding God Through My Patients*, RRP International Publishing, LLC, 2015.

Santuario de Chimayo, Booklet, www.holychimayo.us.

Shealy, C. Norman, *Miracles Do Happen—A Physician's Experience with Alternative Medicine*, Element Books, Ltd., 1995.

Steiger, Brad and Steiger-Hansen, Sherry, *He Walks With Me—True Encounters with Jesus*, Signet, 1998.

*Tschirhart-Sanford, Linda and Donovan, Ellen, *Women and Self-Esteem*, Penguin Books, 1984.

Walsch, Neale Donald, *Conversations with God: An Uncommon Dialogue*, Penguin Group, USA, Inc., 1996.

About the Author

Author/Healer Diana Michael lives in Coon Rapids, Minnesota with her husband Bill. She has one son Kenneth Dean. Her first published book received a true story movie option. She has been doing energy healing for nearly thirty years volunteering at Pathways Health Crisis Resource Center, Unity North Spiritual Center, and the Virginia Piper Cancer Institute. She works as a medical transcriptionist for MHVI, a local cardiology group. Diana's intention is to renew hope and save someone's life as hers was so mercifully spared against all odds.

After being raped at age sixteen, Diana takes an overdose and has a near death experience. Angels rescue her and promise to protect her, asking her to tell the truth. Television celebrity Steve Allen intervenes saving Diana's life with uncanny synchronicity, beginning an enduring friendship. Against her will, in a comedy of errors, the angels kept their promise to protect her from suicide, murder, domestic abuse and cancer. Diana is guided to powerful psychics, shamans, ministers and spiritual healers who renew her faith in the Divine. She is witness to spirit visitations, angelic rescues, and miraculous healings. The intensity of her harrowing journey is balanced with love, forgiveness, and a surprising sense of humor. This true story, making light of the spiritual journey, is written in return for the Promise of Angels.

DianaMichael.author@outlook.com